# ECHO BEACH

# ECHO BEACH
## *SEOHAE MON AMOUR*

David Kent

Pedagogy Press

**Copyright © 2020 David Kent.
All rights reserved.**

No part of this publication may be reproduced, distributed, or transmitted in any form or by any means, including photocopying, recording, or other electronic or mechanical methods, without prior written permission.

All photographs were taken on an iPhone of objects in place. Any discarded items photographed were disposed of properly where possible. The photographs do not depict any one beach in particular. All images were taken at a number of locations along the western shores of the Republic of Korea throughout 2018 and 2019.

These curated images serve to represent a composite of Korean beach culture at one specific point in time.

**Cover images:** Water's edge, Here, buoy! (David Kent).

**Korean translation:** 선현희 (Son Hyunhee).

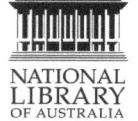 A catalogue record for this book is available from the National Library of Australia

ISBN: 9781925555462

*Pedagogy Press*
www.pedagogypress.com

Sydney, Australia.

First Edition.

# CONTENTS

**Acknowledgements** — vii

**Echo Beach** — 1
   *Seohae Mon Amour* — 2

**1 Quiescence** — 4
   *Float with me, Safety in numbers, Shaken, not stirred, My island home, 80,000 leagues, There must be some way outta here, Caged.*

**2 Go-Stop** — 11
   *Godori.*

**3 Sand Toys** — 12
   *Chilly crab, Dump truck 1, Dump truck 2, Hatchling, Beached whale, Pine mahal, The missing piece.*

**4 Fire Flowers** — 20
   *Smoke flower, Wish I may, wish I might, Brass.*

**5 People** — 24
   *Camelot, Solitude sits, Couple sits, Solitary couples, Solitude walks, Solitude feeds, Solitude beckons, Couple do, Couple look.*

**6 An Industry** — 34
   *Trigger, Urban waterfalls, Lure of the wild, Here, buoy!, Pagoda with a view, 3-hour tour, S. S. Minnow, Rescue 13, Baywatch, Paddy wagon 119, Lifesaver, Solitary man, Dead weight, Safe harbor, Water's edge, Pier's end, Throw a shrimp in yellow wine.*

**7 Tourist Traps** — 48
   *Stairway to heaven, Mud girl, I'm melting, Sold out, Beach mascot 1, Golden arches, GS25, soft-shell clam and tram, Plastic pools, Tidal pools, Farm fresh, Brevi herbae aere impleta supernatet, King hit, Barrel ride, The beginning, Tower of travel, Caught in the undertow, Safe water, Overflight, On the rocks, Road to nowhere.*

**8 Ecology** — 64
   *Crab, Dolmon, The birds, Fantasy Island, Keeled over, LB – Lucky Bluestar, Cuttlefish, Lifelines, Shell shock, Cold feet, Tetraodontidae with kelp and shells on sand, Flagellation, Tunnel vision, … full of grace.*

**9 Refuse** — 79
   *Refuse no. 10, Mommy's hand, Ramyeon, Watermelon sugar, Elixirs of life, Thirst, YehShen's slipper, Myopia, Band of brothers, Smoko, Supercalifragilisticexpialidocious, For cup's sake, Daddy's hand, Squid.*

**About the Photographer** — 93

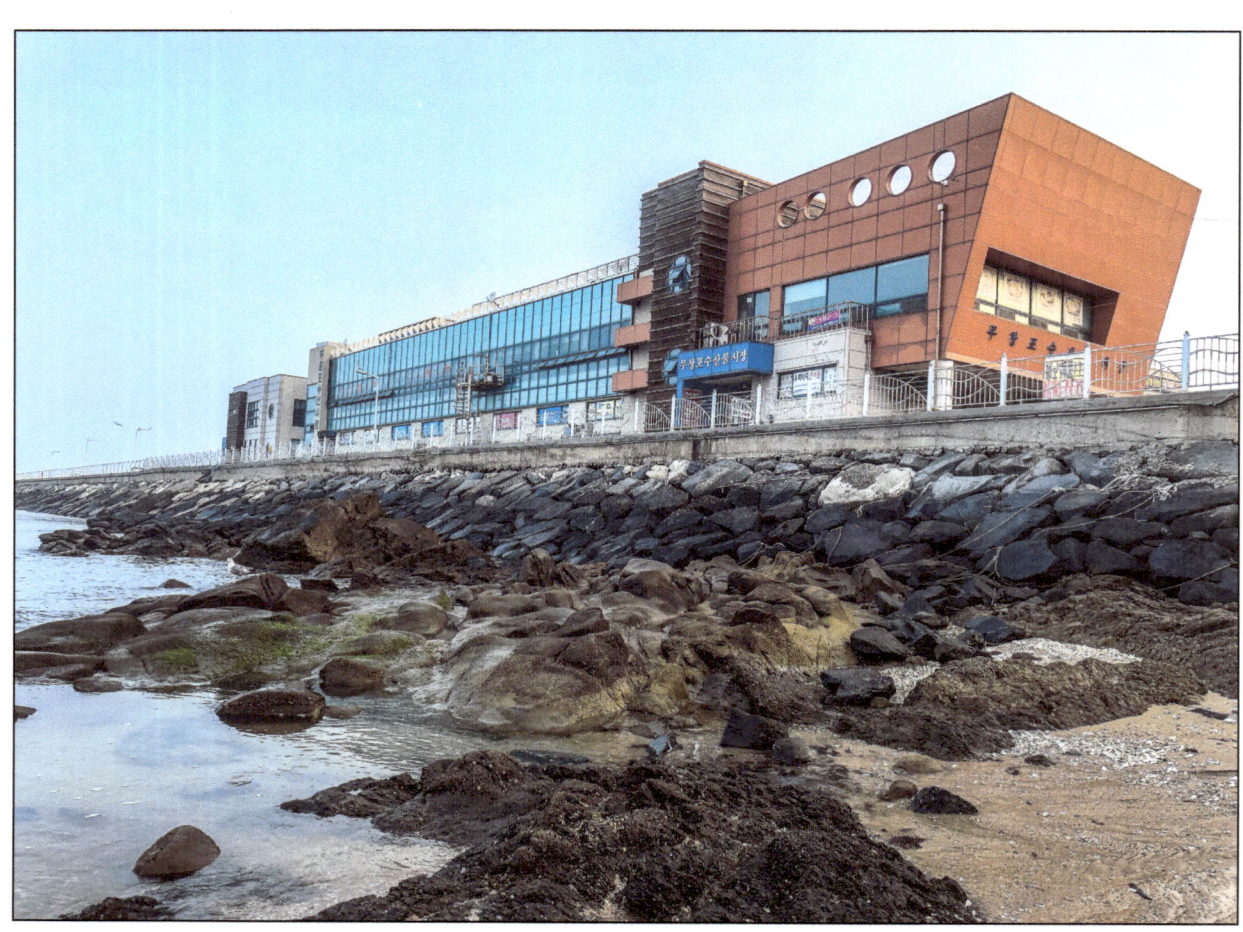

*Fish mongers*
생선 가게

# ACKNOWLEDGEMENTS

Special thanks to *Christopher Maslon* for his encouragement, vision, and exceptional advice, and to the *Daejon Arts Collective (DJAC)* for their inspiration. I would also like to extend my deepest appreciation to my wife *Hyunhee* who has been very patient and understanding throughout the entire process involved with the curation of these images and to thank her for lending her remarkable translation skills to this project.

## 감사의 말

저에게 격려와 통찰 및 훌륭한 자문을 준 Christopher Maslon 과 영감을 준 대전국제예술가모임(DJAC)에 특별한 감사를 드립니다. 또한 이 이미지들을 기획 구상하는데 필요한 모든 과정 내내 인내심을 갖고 이해해 준 아내 현희에게 깊은 감사를 표하고 이 프로젝트의 번역을 해줘서 감사 드립니다.

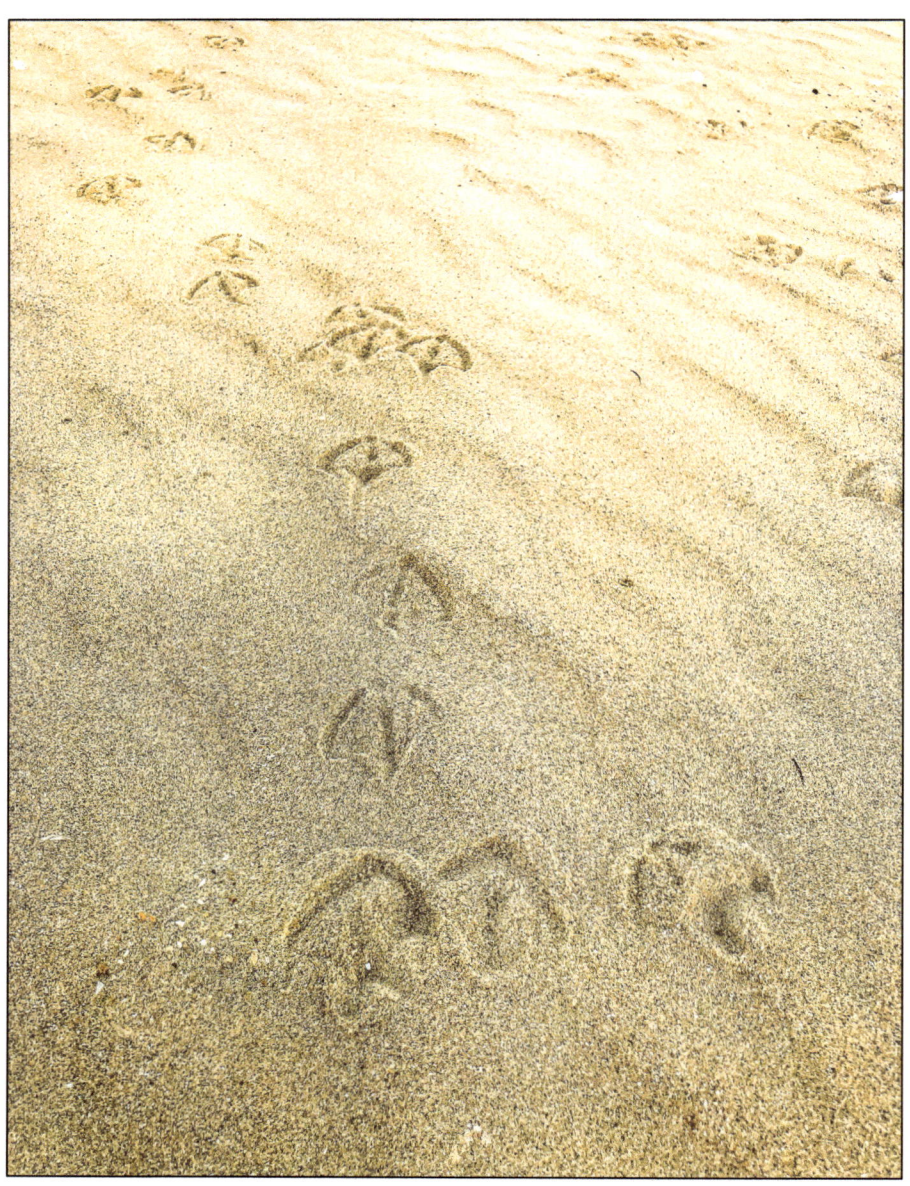

*Footprints in the sand*
모래 위 발자국

# Echo Beach

*Echo Beach* is a fictional beach that resides along the western coast of the Korean peninsula. For those land-locked in cities and tied to the long hours of work and domestic duties, it is a place of fantasy. In reality, it may also be a beach they love and one that they may never get to visit, remaining far away in time.

For some it may be a shoreline that conjures up thoughts, desires, and expectations of a long-awaited summer vacation, the notion of fun with family, and a time to relax and enjoy life. For others, it may be a place where worries can be cast to the wind, pain can be swallowed into the depths of the sea, sorrows can sink into the sand, and they can take solace in solitude.

Aside from the fantasy and the imagery that *Echo Beach* brings to mind, and the desire and pull it has for city-dwellers, the images* chosen for this collection are those that stand, perhaps, in stark contrast to the above. They do this by not only illustrating how the reality of this fantasy and desire may play out, but the reality of what it must play out alongside – the flotsam and jetsam of refuse.

*All images were taken on an iPhone of people and objects in place. Any discarded items photographed were disposed of properly where possible.

에코 비치는 남한의 서해안을 따라 존재하는 허구의 해변입니다. 도시에 둘러싸여 장시간의 업무와 국내 업무에 묶여있는 사람들에게, 이곳은 환상의 장소입니다. 실제로, 이곳은 또한 사람들이 사랑하는 해변일지도 모릅니다. 그리고 이곳은 결국 먼 곳으로 남은 채, 결코 방문할 수 없는 해변일 수도 있습니다.

어떤 사람들에게 이곳은 오랫동안 기다려 왔던 여름 휴가의 생각, 욕망, 기대, 가족과의 즐거움, 휴식을 취하며 인생을 즐길 수 있는 시간을 떠올리게 하는 해안선이 될 수도 있습니다. 또 다른 사람들에게 이곳은 걱정을 바람에 내던지고, 고통이 바다 깊숙이 삼켜지게, 슬픔은 모래 속으로 가라앉을 수 있는 곳이며 그들이 고독을 위안으로 삼을 수 있는 장소일지도 모릅니다.

에코 비치(Echo Beach)가 떠올리게 하는 환상과 이미지, 그리고 도시 거주자들에 대한 열망과 매력을 제외하고 이 전시회를 위해 선택된 사진*은 아마, 위와 극명하게 대조가 되는 것들입니다. 이것들은 이 환상과 욕망의 현실이 어떻게 전개될 수 있는지를 보여줄 뿐만 아니라, 그것이 함께 일어나야만 하는 현실-쓰레기의 표류물과 해양폐기물을 보여줌으로써 이것을 합니다.

*모든 이미지는 제자리에 있는 사람과 물체를 iPhone 으로 촬영된 것입니다. 사진에 찍힌 모든 버려진 물건은 가능한 곳에 적절하게 처리되었습니다.

# *Seohae Mon Amour*

The West Sea, *Seohae* (서해) as it is known to Koreans, is located between mainland China and the Korean Peninsula. The sea bottom and shores are dominated by silt and sand brought to the region by rivers through the Bohai Sea and the Korea Bay. It is these deposits, along with sand particles coming into the region as a result of Gobi Desert sand storms, that are responsible for coloring the water a golden hue, and hence it is also known as *Hwangehae* (황해), the Yellow Sea.

The major South Korean ports on this sea are Incheon, Gunsan, and Mokpo, and that for North Korea is Nampo (the outer port of the capital Pyongyang). Since November 01, 2018 the Yellow Sea has served as the location of 'peace zones' between North and South Korea with a buffer zone created along the Northern Limit Line (NLL).

On-shore Korean summer temperatures range from 22 to 28°C (72 to 82°F), and it is a wet and warm time with frequent typhoons from June through October. Winters are cold and dry. Tides are semidiurnal (i.e., rising twice a day), with an amplitude of 4 to 8 meters (13 to 26 feet), with maximum heights occurring in the spring. Tide-related sea variations allow for a 10 to 40 meter (33 to 131 foot) wide opening between two islands (Jindo and Modo) to occur for approximately one hour at the beginning of May and the middle of June each year.

The entire west coast of Korea contains a 10 kilometer wide (6.2 mile) belt of intertidal mudflats, which has a total area of 2,850 square kilometers (1,100 square miles). These mudflats are of great importance to migratory waders and shorebirds as they contain sediment-rich benthic fauna. A minimum of two million birds pass through the area northward, and about half that number use it for southward migration. It is, therefore, the single most important site for migratory birds on their northward movement across the entire East Asian – Australasian Flyway.

Today, the coasts of the Yellow Sea are densely populated, and it has become one of the most degraded marine areas on earth. Coastal destruction is being led by agriculture, aquaculture, and industrial development. The ecosystem is endangered. Biodiversity, fisheries, and ecosystem services are in decline. Pollution is widespread.

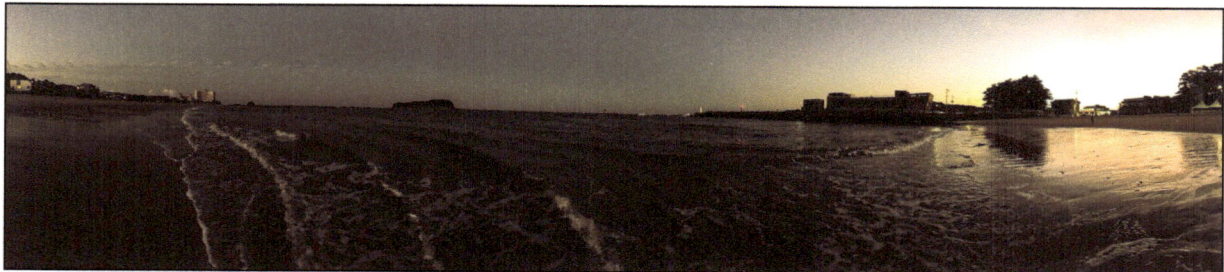

*June bloom*
6월의 만개

*Seohae Mon Amour*

# 서해 내 사랑

한국인에게 서해(Seohea)라고 알려진 이곳 서해안은 중국 본토와 한반도 사이에 위치해 있습니다. 해저와 해안은 보하이(Bohai)해와 한국만(Korea Bay)를 통해 강가 지역으로 운반된 미사와 모래가 대부분입니다. 고비사막 모래 폭풍의 결과로 모래 입자가 이 지역에 유입되면서 이 퇴적물이 물을 황금색으로 물들이는 역할을 합니다. 그 결과 이곳은 또한 황해(Hwangehae)로 알려져 있습니다.

이 해안의 주요 항구는 인천, 군산, 목포이고 북한은 남포 (수도인 평양 외곽 항구)입니다. 2018 년 11 월 1 일 이후, 황해는 북한계선(Northern Limit Line, NLL)을 따라 형성된 완충지대로 남북한 사이에 '평화 지대'라는 장소의 역할을 합니다.

한국의 육지 여름 기온은 섭씨 22~28 도 (화씨 72~82 도) 사이이며, 6 월에서 10 월까지는 잦은 태풍이 발생하여 습하고 따뜻한 날씨이나 겨울은 춥고, 건조합니다. 조수는 4~8m (13~26 피트)의 진폭으로 봄에 최대 높이가 발생하며 반일(즉 하루 2 회 상승)입니다. 조수와 관련된 바다의 변화는 두 섬(진도와 모도) 사이에 폭 10~40m (33-131 피트)로 바다 갈라짐이 매년 5 월 초와 6 월 중순에 약 1 시간 동안 일어나게 합니다.

한국의 서해안 전체에는 10km 너비 (6.2 마일)의 조간대 갯벌이 있으며 총면적은 2,850km2 (1,100 제곱마일)입니다. 이 갯벌은 침전물이 풍부한 저서 동물상을 포함하고 있어서 섭금류와 도요새·물떼새류에게 매우 중요합니다. 최소 2 백만 마리의 새가 북쪽 지역을 통과하고 그 중 약 절반은 남쪽으로 이주하는 데 이곳을 사용합니다. 그래서 이곳은 동아시아-오스트랄라시아(오스트레일리아·뉴질랜드·서남 태평양 제도를 포함하는 지역) 경로 전역을 거쳐 북쪽으로 이동하는 철새들에게 가장 중요한 단일 장소입니다.

오늘날 황해 연안은 인구 밀도가 높고 지구상에서 가장 퇴화한 해양 지역 중 하나가 되었습니다. 해안 파괴는 농업, 수경재배 및 산업 개발에 의해 진행되고 있고. 생태계는 위험에 처해있습니다. 생물 다양성, 어업 및 생태계 서비스가 감소하고 있으며, 오염은 널리 퍼져 있습니다.

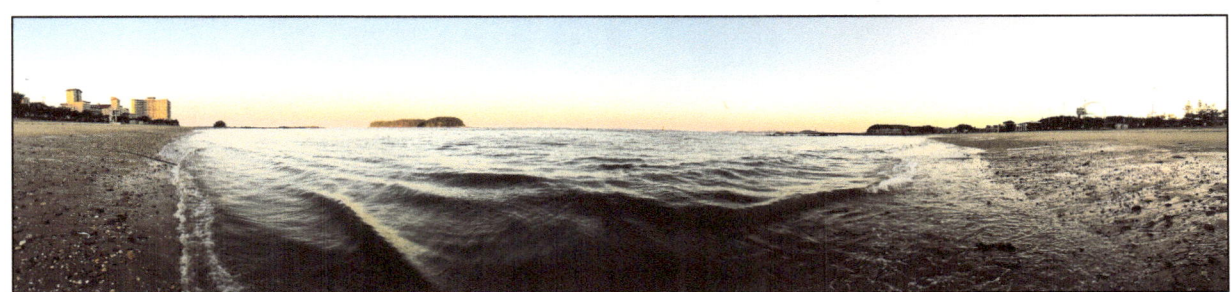

*September sunrise*
9 월의 해돋이

# Quiescence

Beachside inflatables in the Republic of Korea are a common sight. They can be rented by the hour, often along with a parasol and use of a locker for storing valuables. Raised rest platforms are also common. These are decks large enough to accommodate a family, and designed to easily allow for the enjoyment of eating a communal meal, playing a game of go-stop (고스톱), or having a drink or two while partaking of a variety of side dishes, and perhaps also indulging in the taste of tobacco from a slender-rolled cigarette.

# 정지

한국의 해변가에 있는 공기 주입식 용품들은 흔한 광경입니다. 그것들은 종종 파라솔과 귀중품을 보관할 수 있는 사물함 이용과 더불어 시간제로 대여가 가능합니다. 휴식을 위해 세워진 단상 또한 여기서는 흔합니다. 그것들은 한 가족을 수용하기에 충분한 크기의 데크(갑판)이며 공동 식사하기, 고스톱(go-stop) 치기 또는 다양한 반찬을 먹으며 음료 한두 잔 마시는 즐거움을 고려해 고안되었고 아마도 가늘게 만 궐련의 담배 맛에 빠질 수 있게도 설계되었습니다.

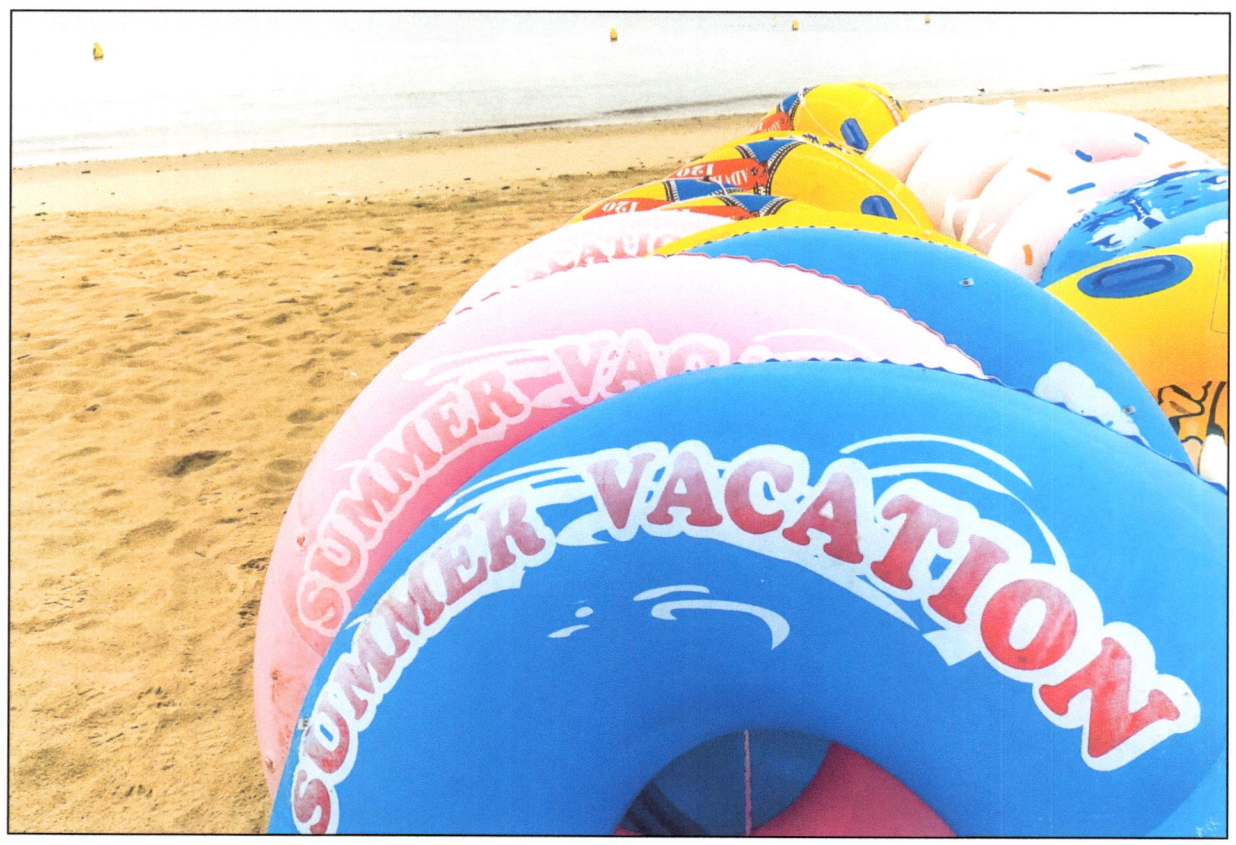

*Float with me*
나와 함께 흘러가다

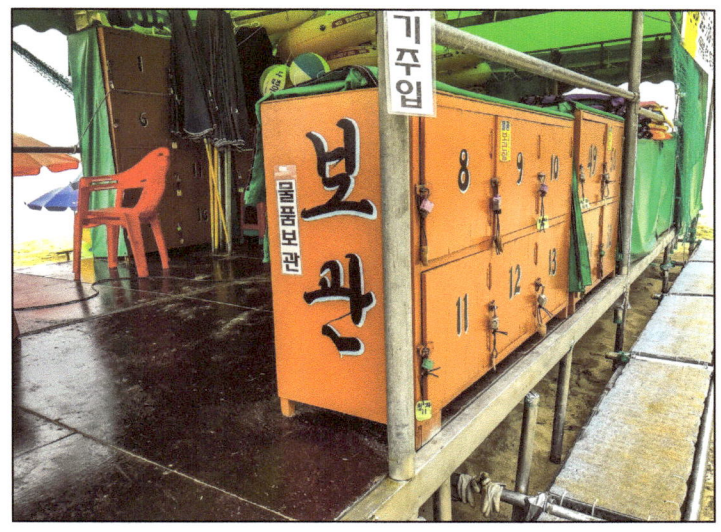

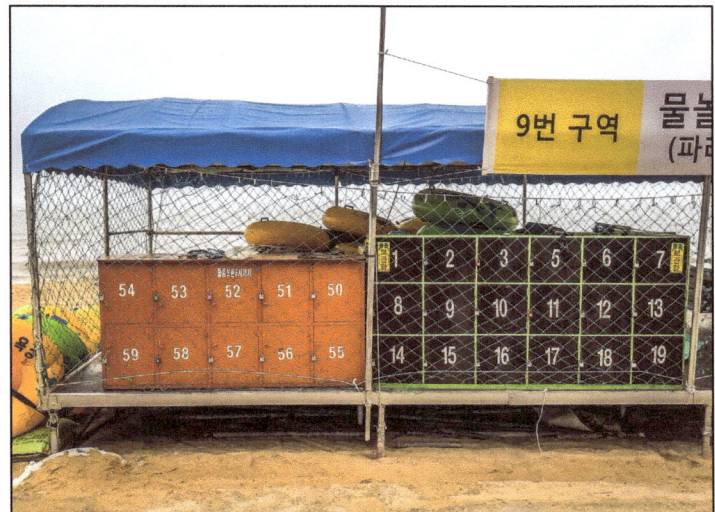

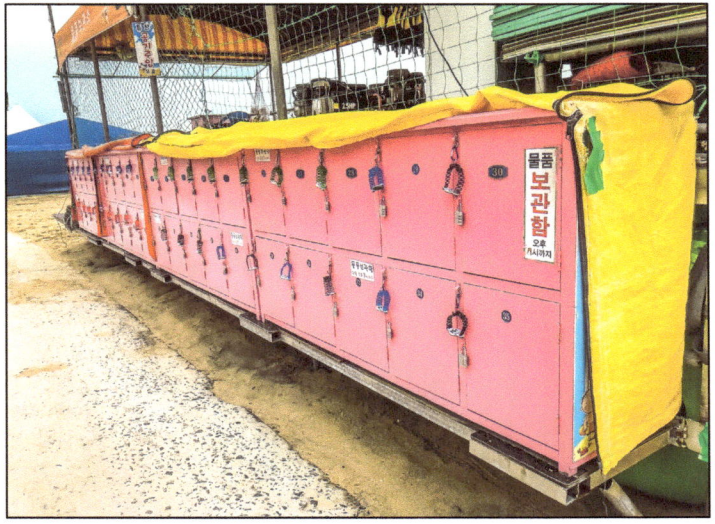

*Safety in numbers*
수가 많은 편이 안전함

# Echo Beach

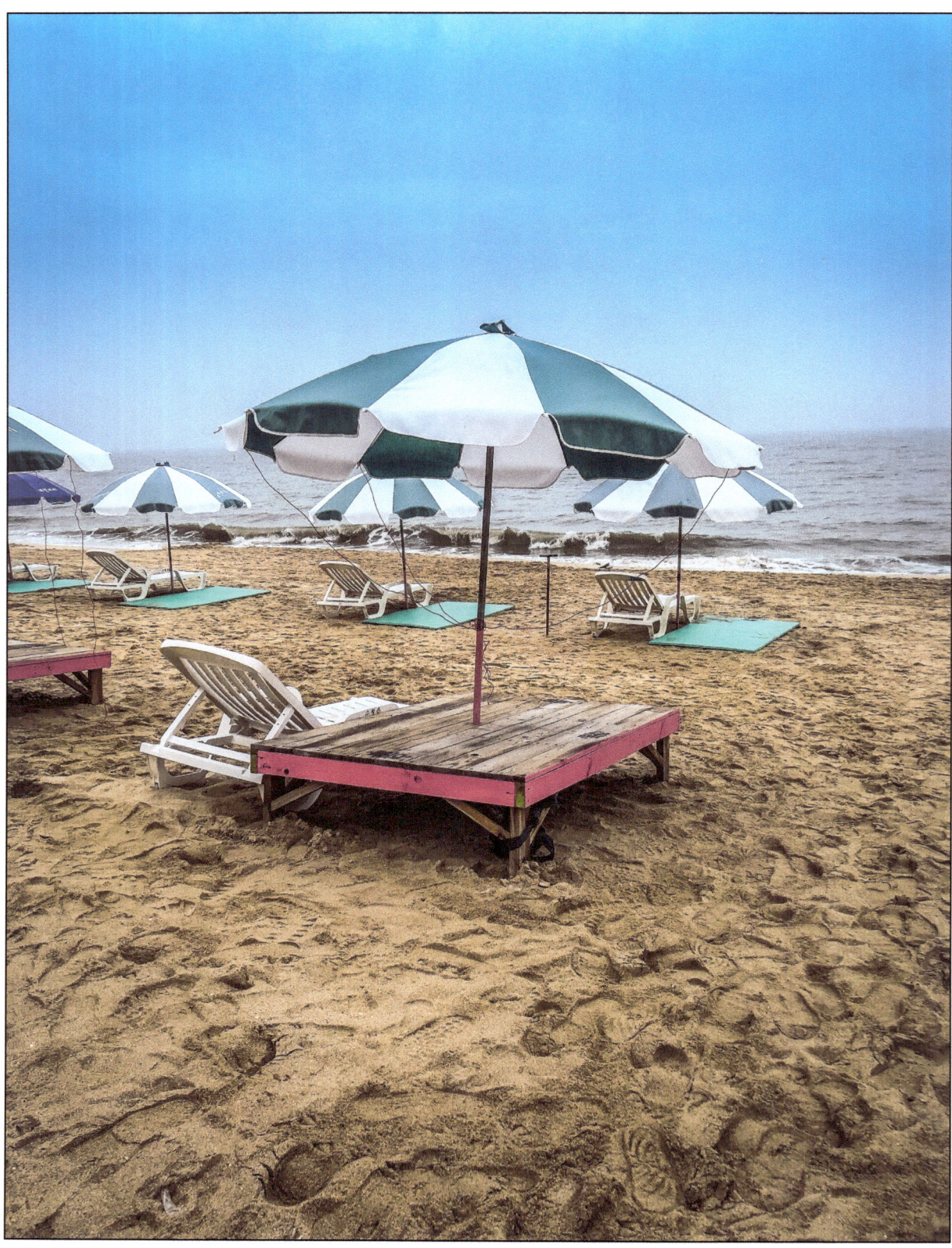

*Shaken, not stirred*
젖지말고 흔들어서

*Seohae Mon Amour*

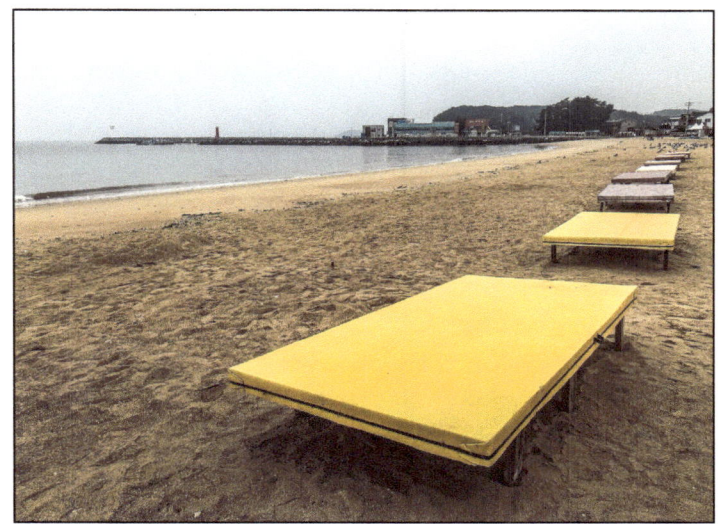

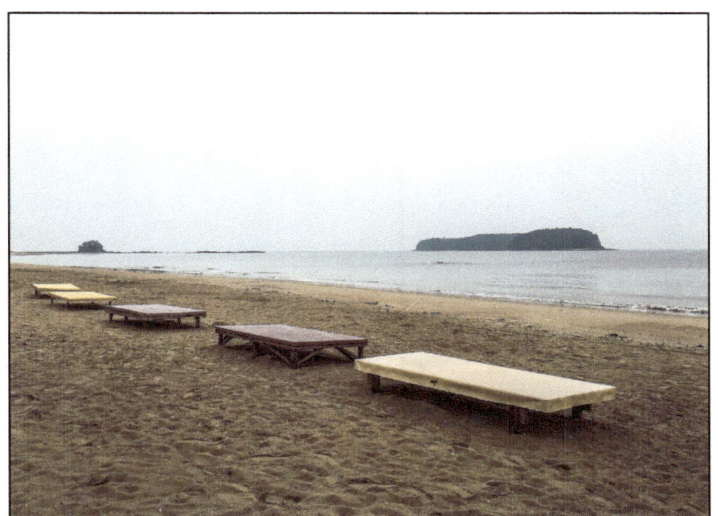

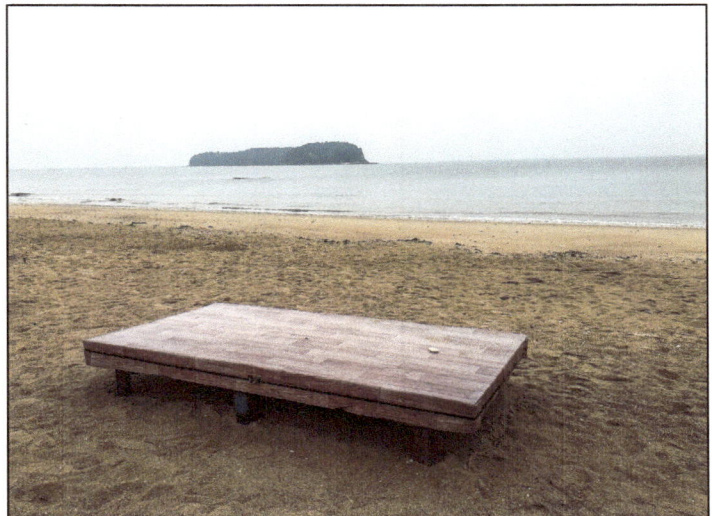

*My island home*
내 섬 집

Echo Beach

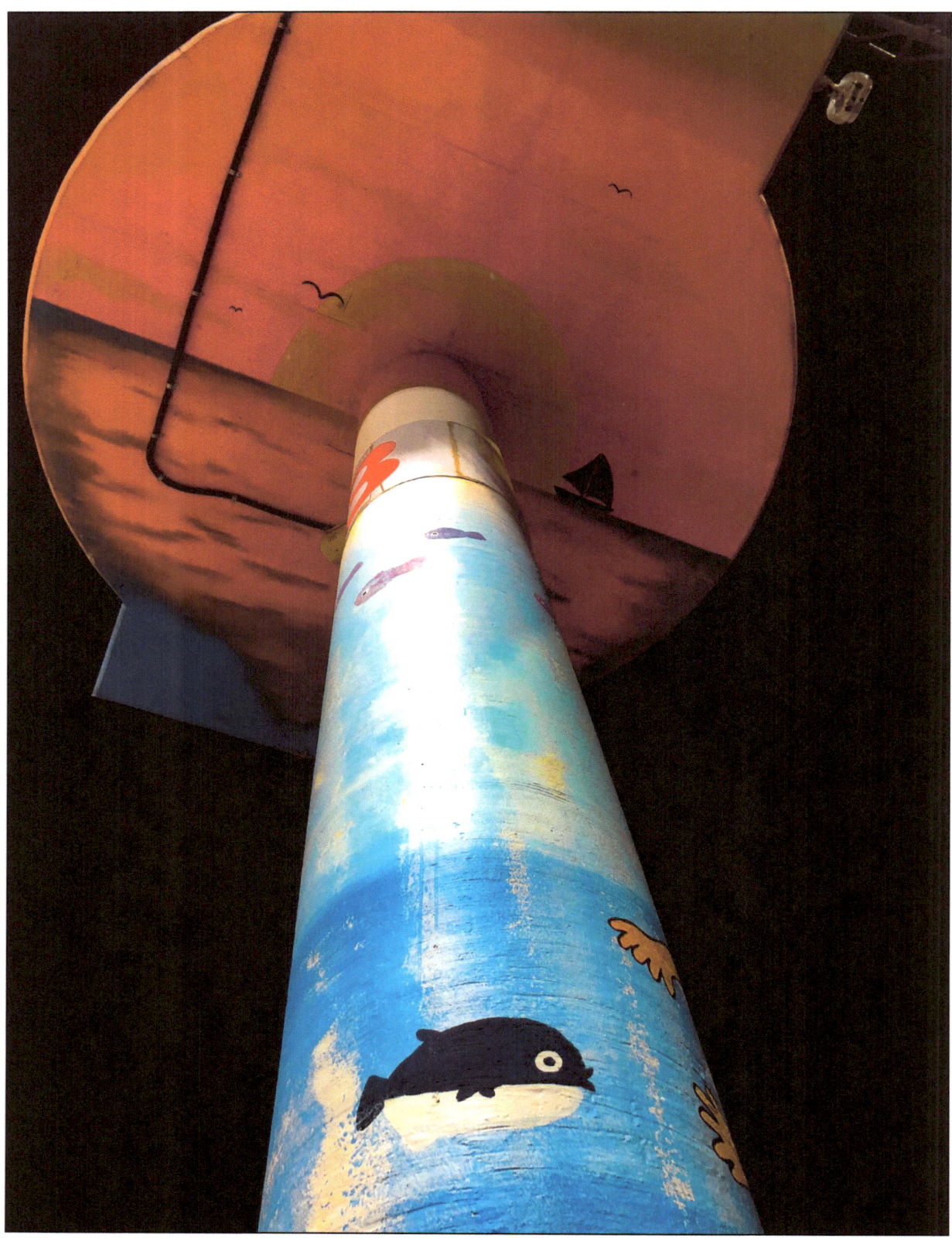

*80,000 leagues*
80,000 개의 리그

*Seohae Mon Amour*

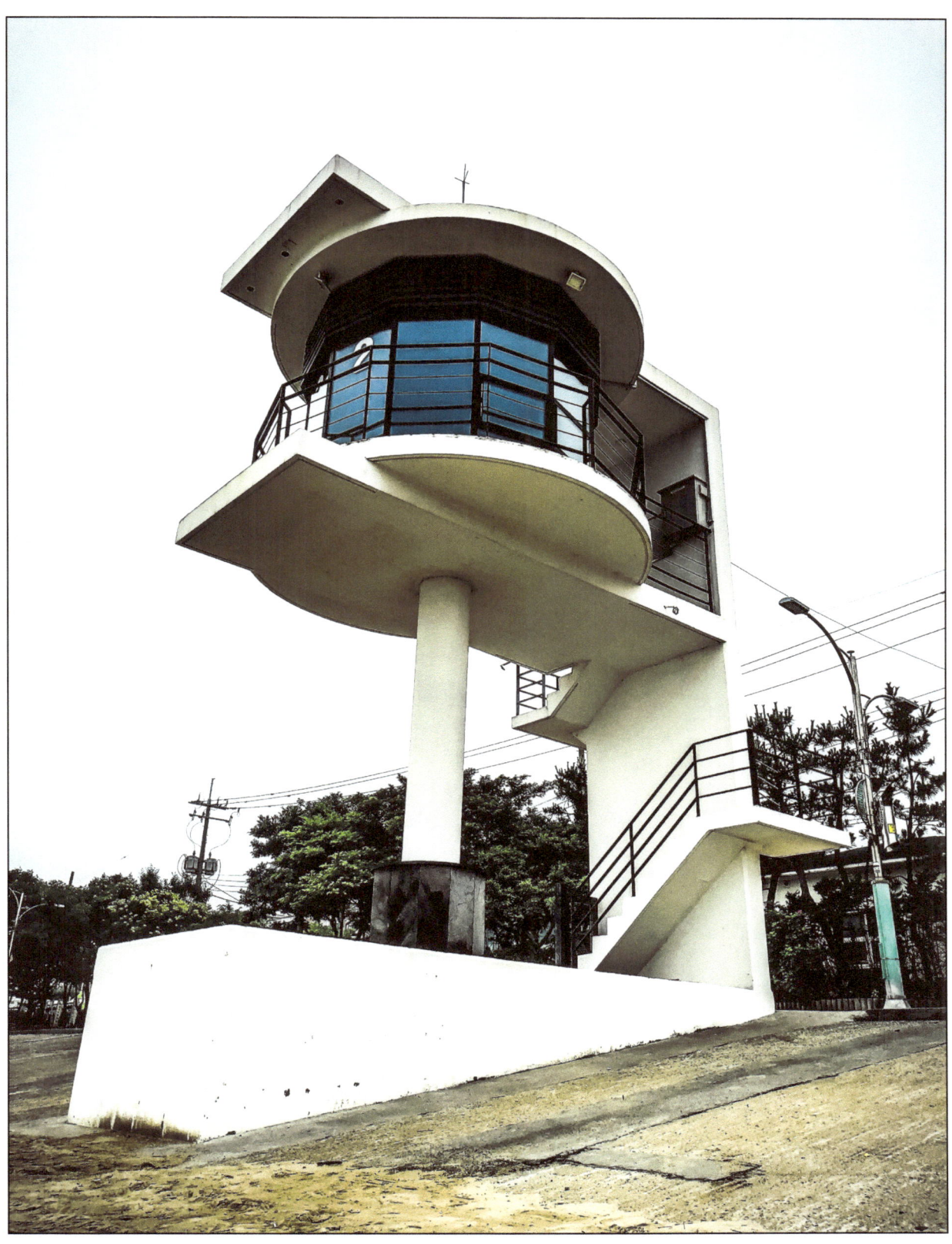

*There must be some kind of way outta here …*
분명 이곳을 빠져나갈 방법이 있을 거야 …

# Echo Beach

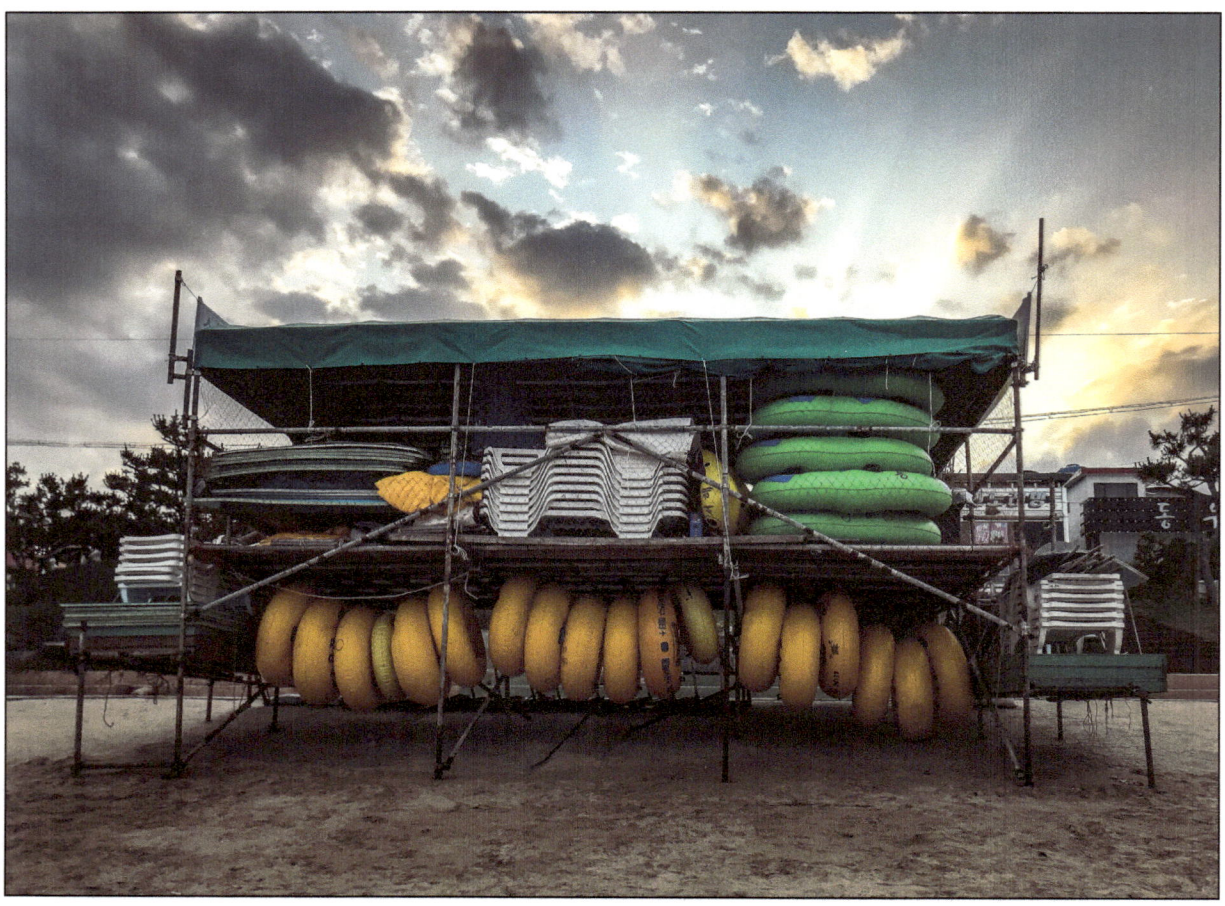

*Caged*
갇힌

# Go-Stop

*Go-Stop* (고스톱), also called *Godori* (고도리) after the winning move in the game, is a Korean card game. It is known as *Matgo* (맞고) when played by only two, or *Hwatu* (화투), the name of the cards themselves. There are typically two to three players, but a fourth can join. The objective of play is to score a minimum predetermined number of points (e.g., a three or a seven), and then call for either a 'go' or a 'stop.' If a 'go' is called, then the game continues with the number of points or the amount of money being played for increased. The risk in this move is that it allows the potential of another player scoring the minimum and wining all of the points or money for themselves. If a 'stop' has been called the game ends, and the caller can collect any winnings.

# 고스톱

게임에서 이길 수 있는 수가 된 후 또한 고도리(Godori)라 불리는 고스톱(Go-Stop)은 한국의 카드놀이입니다. 두 명이 만 하는 고스톱을 맞고(Matgo)라 부르고 화투(Hwatu)는 카드 자체의 이름입니다. 일반적으로 2~3명이 할 수 있지만 네 번째 참여자도 동참할 수 있습니다. 놀이의 목적은 최소 점수 (예를 들어, 3 또는 7)을 낸 후, 고 또는 스톱을 외치는 것입니다. 고가 외쳐지면 게임은 해당 게임에서 난 점수나 판돈이 증가하여 계속 진행됩니다. 이 수의 위험은 또 다른 참여자가 최소 점수를 내면 모든 점수나 판돈을 가져갈 수 있는 가능성을 허용한다는 것입니다. 스톱이 외쳐지면 해당 게임은 끝나고 스톱을 외친 사람이 모든 돈을 가져갈 수 있습니다.

고    도    리

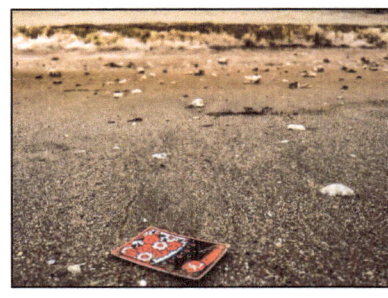 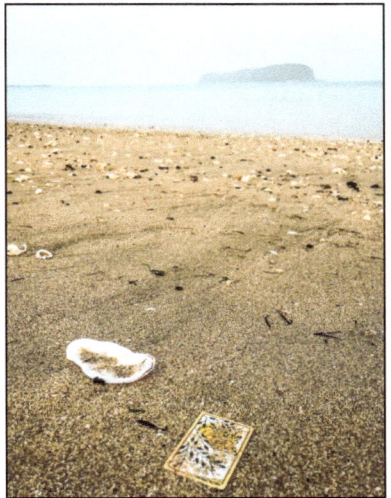 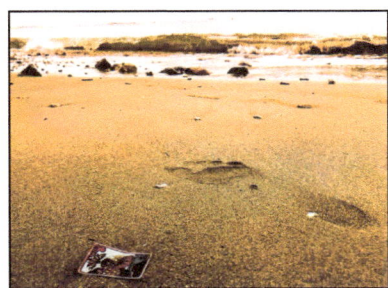

*Godori*
고도리

## Sand Toys

Since the 1920s South Korea has celebrated Children's Day, becoming a national holiday (held on May 05) from the 1970s. On this day families often do something special, taking trips to places such as amusement parks, zoos, arboretums or the beach. Parents may also treat their children to snacks, ice cream or a new toy. Playing with sand toys at the beach can be an enjoyable and engaging experience for children. Play can cultivate creativity while developing dexterity and imagination, and it can improve the cognitive, emotional, and physical strength of children as well.

## 모래 장난감

1920 년대 이후 한국은 어린이날을 기념해왔고 1970 년대부터 국경일 (5 월 5 일)이 되었습니다. 가족들은 이날 종종 특별한 것을 하는데 놀이 공원, 동물원, 수목원 또는 해변과 같은 곳으로 여행을 떠납니다. 부모님들은 간식, 아이스크림이나 새 장난감으로 아이들을 특별 대우할지도 모릅니다. 해변에서 모래 장난감을 가지고 노는 것은 아이들에게 즐겁고 매력적인 경험이 될 수 있습니다. 놀이는 손재주와 상상력을 키우며 창의력을 기르고 어린이의 인지력, 정서적, 육체적 힘 또한 기를 수 있게 합니다.

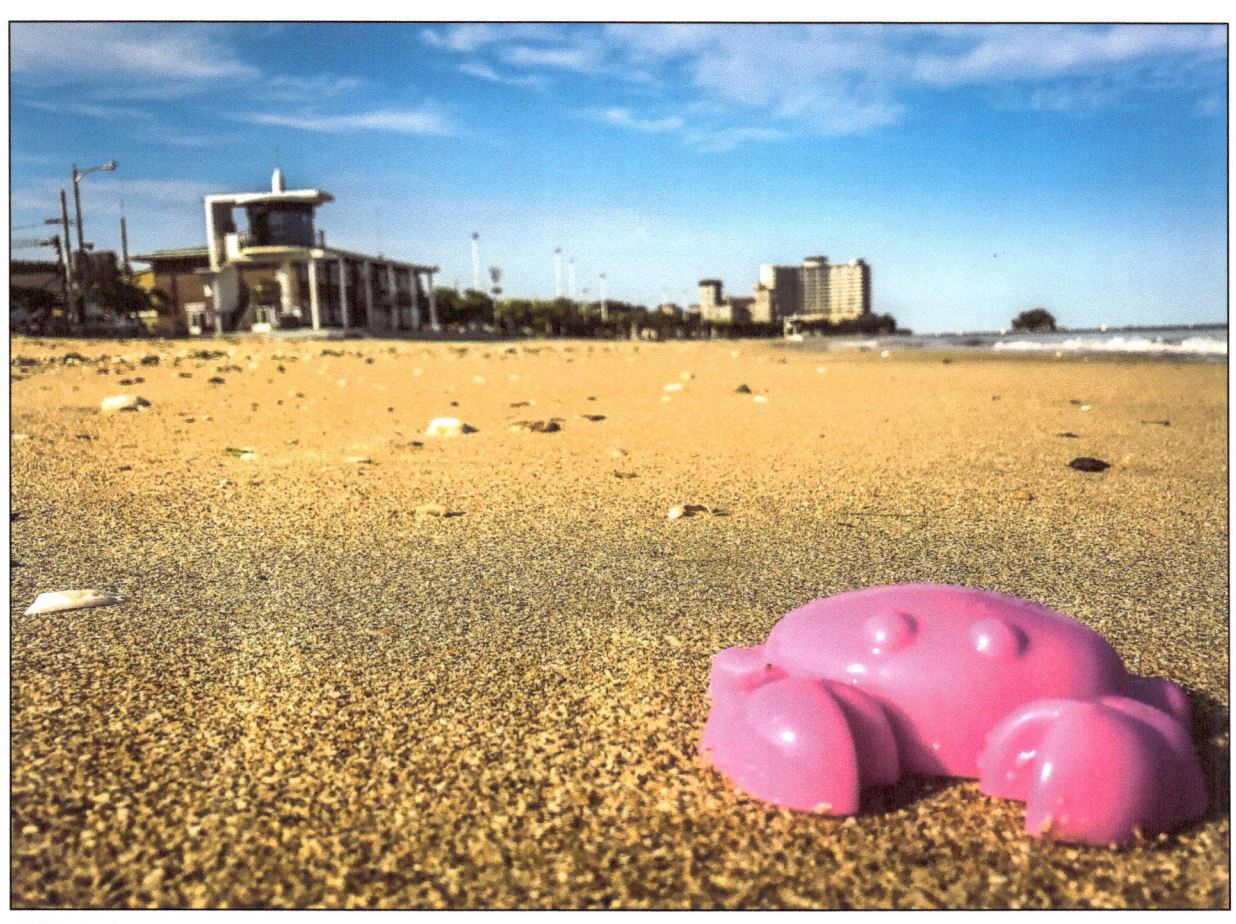

*Chilly Crab*
칠리 크랩

# Echo Beach

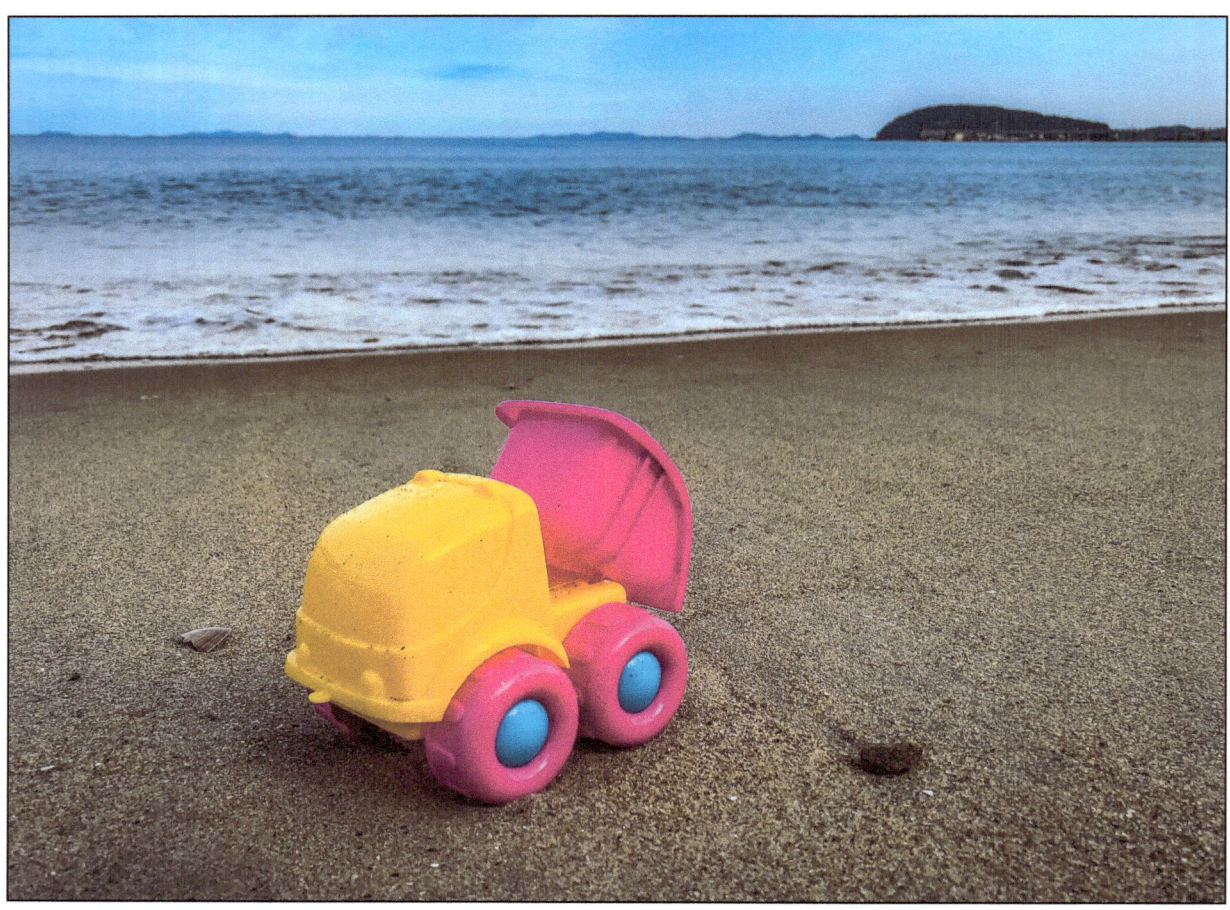

*Dump truck 1*
덤프트럭 1

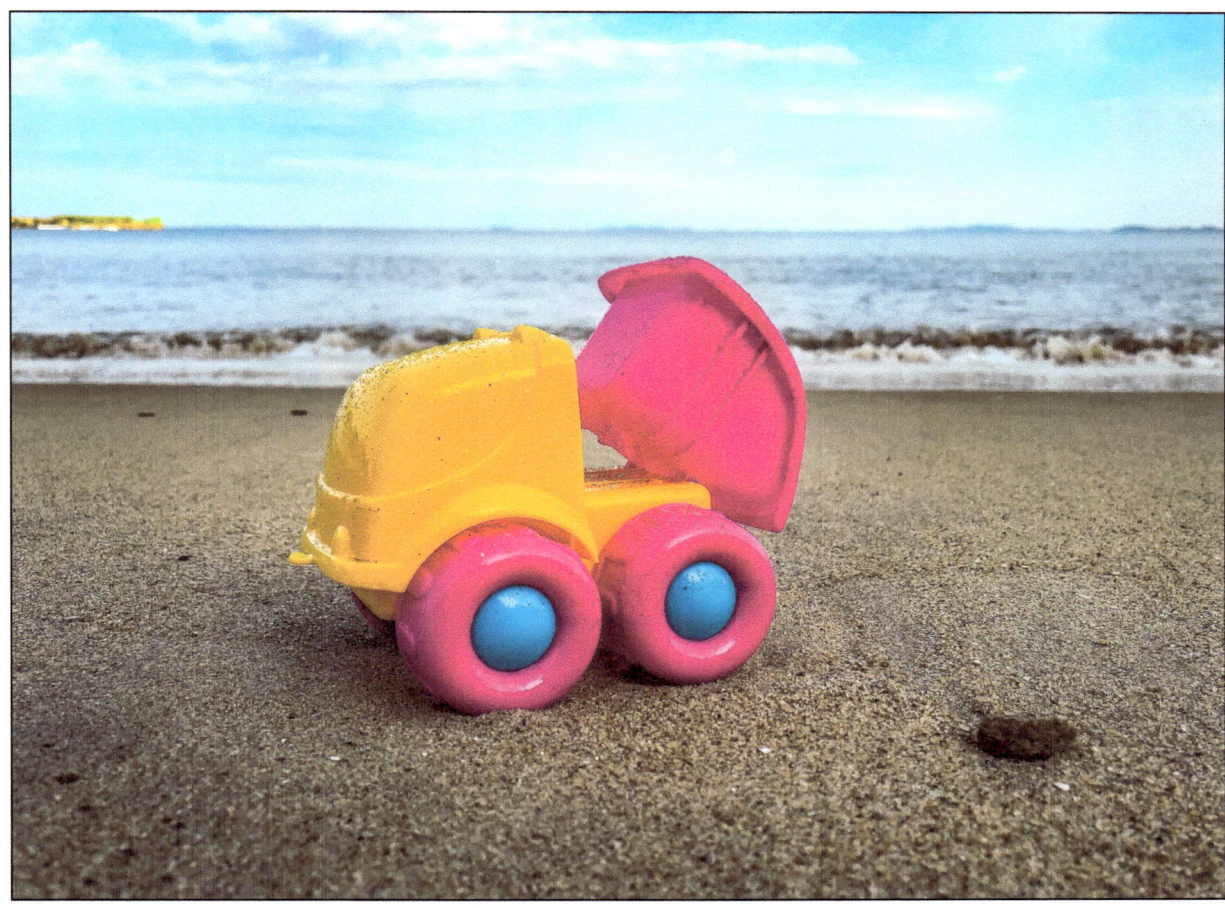

*Dump truck 2*
덤프트럭 2

# Echo Beach

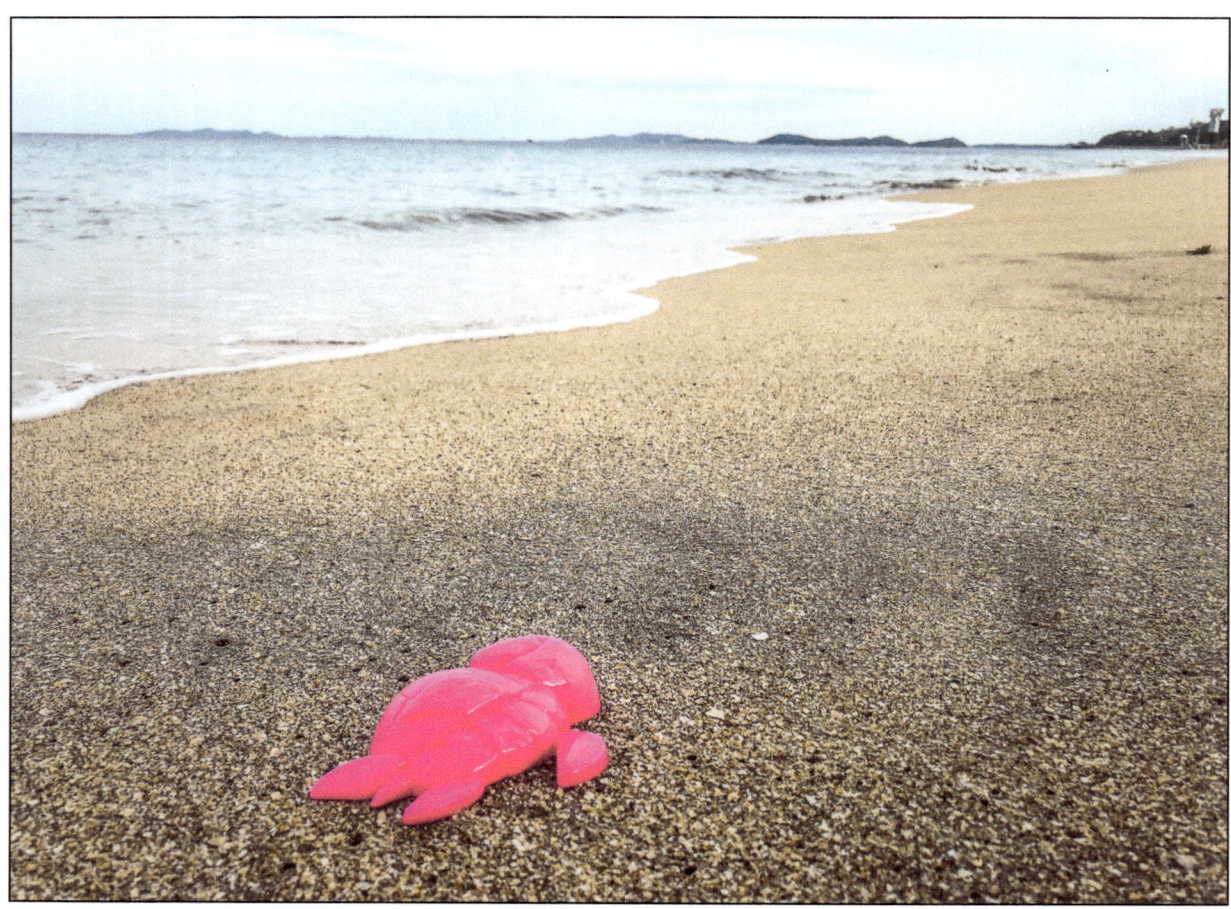

*Hatchling*
갓 부화한 새끼

*Seohae Mon Amour*

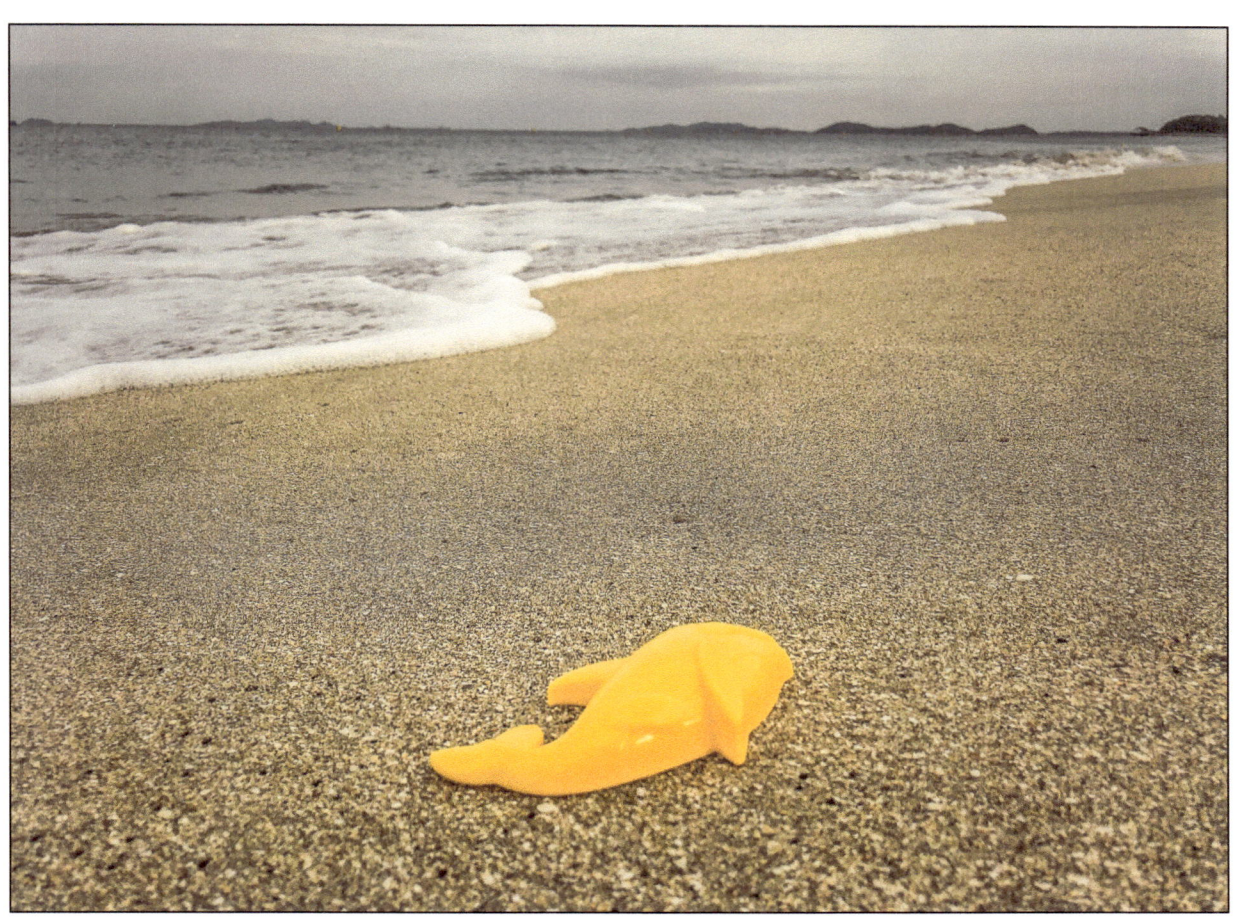

*Beached whale*
해변에 밀려온 고래

# Echo Beach

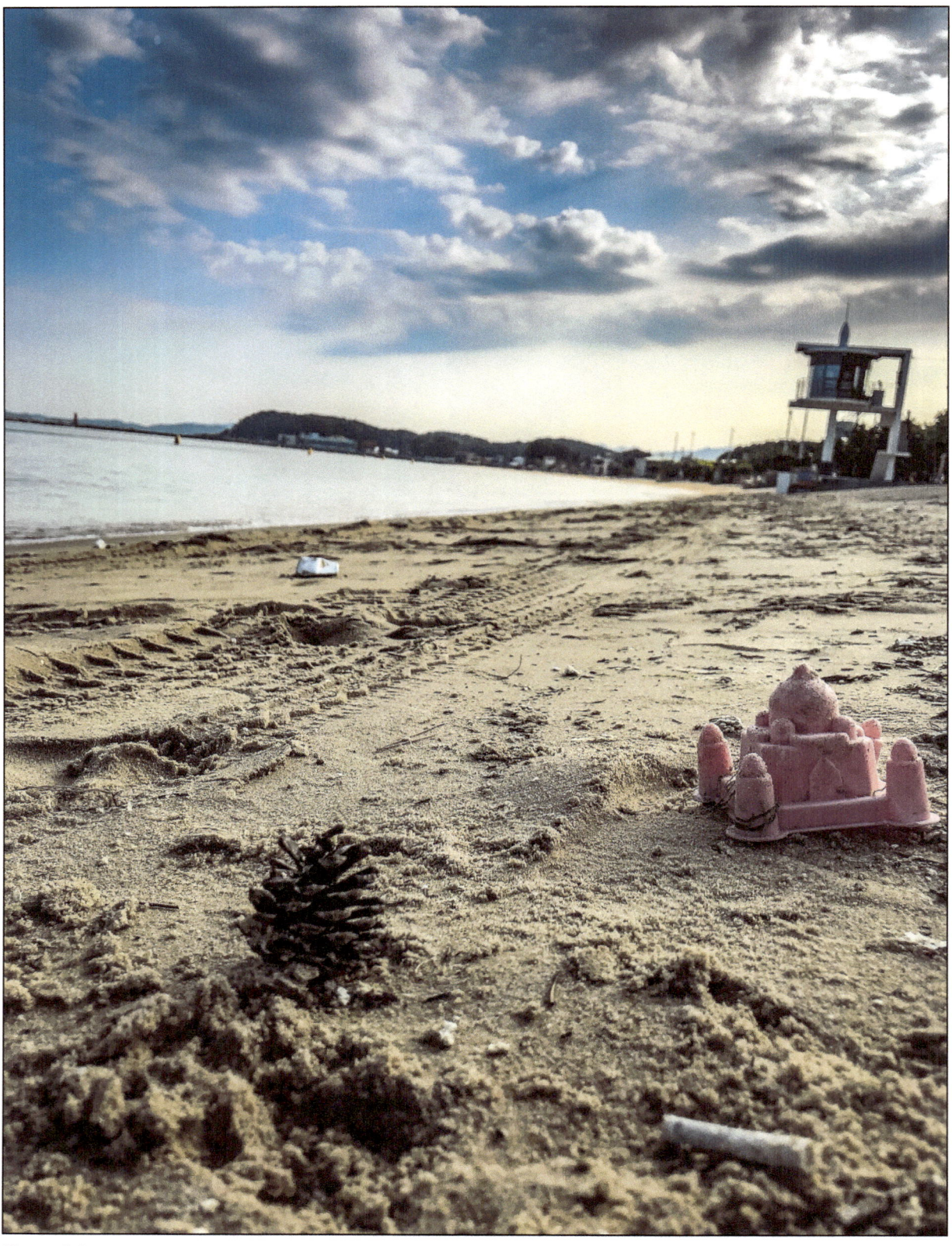

*Pine mahal*
솔방울 궁전

*Seohae Mon Amour*

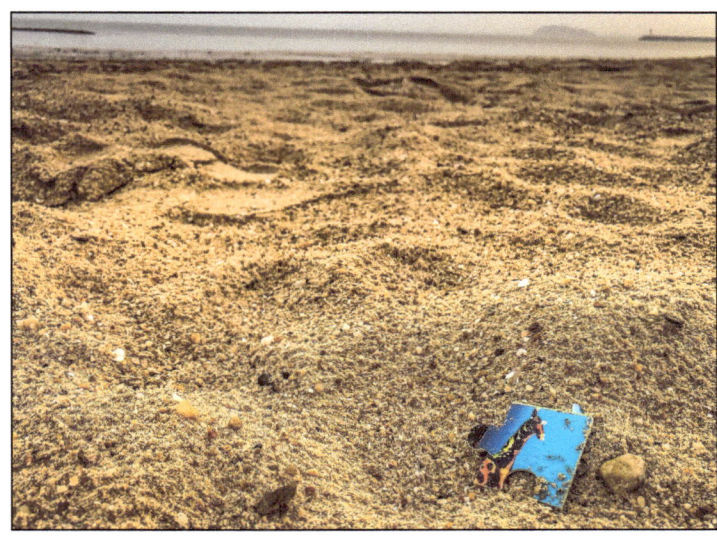

*The missing piece*
잃어버린 조각

# Fire Flowers

*Fire flowers*, or fireworks, play an important role in many cultures and are used to ward off evil spirits or for reasons of celebration and cheer. In South Korea, they can be set off anywhere along the beach. Some fireworks are even handheld, coming in the shape of a gun, and can shoot sparks. Convenience store owners sell them from ₩3,000 (~US$3) and will perhaps be so generous as to lend you a lighter, should you need. Many cities host firework festivals throughout the year including Pohang, on the east coast, which is known as the 'City of Light and Fire.'

# 불꽃

불꽃이나 불꽃놀이는 많은 문화권에서 중요한 역할을 하며 악령을 내쫓거나 축하와 응원의 이유로 사용됩니다. 한국에서는 해변을 따라 어디에서든지 폭죽을 터뜨릴 수 있습니다. 일부 폭죽은 손바닥 크기에 총 모양으로, 불꽃을 쏠 수 있습니다. 편의점 주인은 3,000 원 (3 달러)부터의 폭죽을 판매하며, 필요한 경우 손님에게 라이터를 빌려줄 만큼 관대할 수도 있습니다. 많은 도시가 '빛과 불의 도시'로 알려진 동해안 포항을 포함해 일년 내내 불꽃 축제를 개최합니다.

*Seohae Mon Amour*

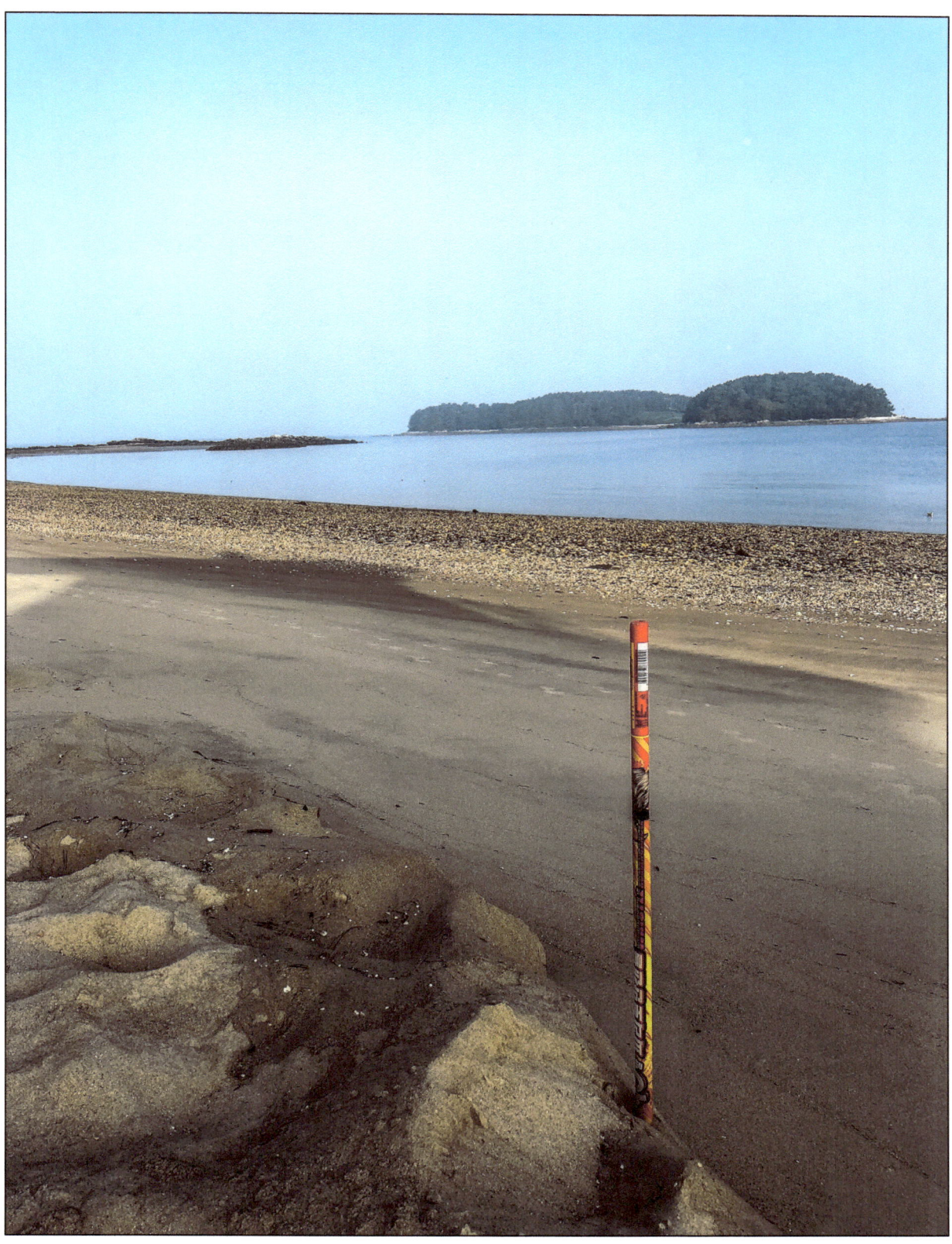

*Smoke flower*
연기 내뿜는 꽃

# Echo Beach

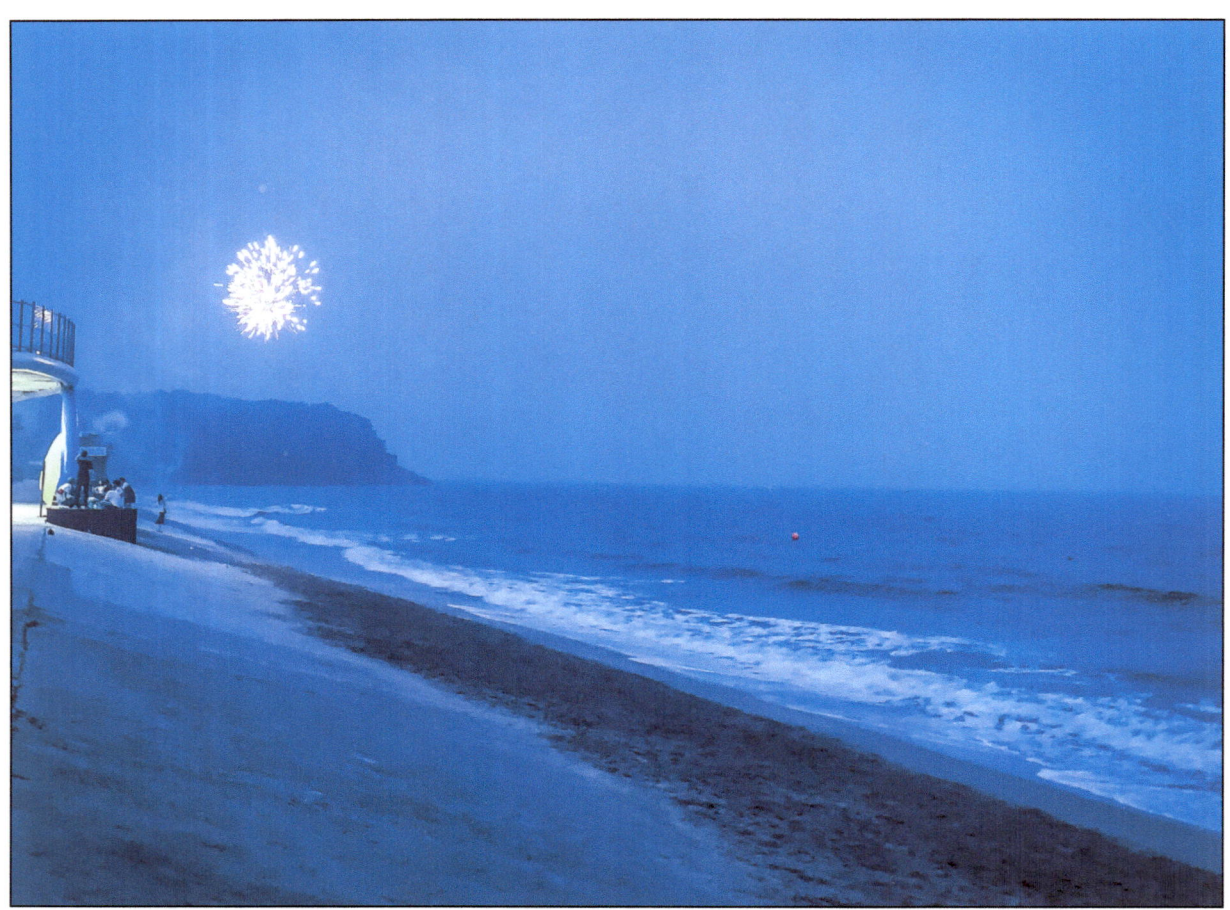

*Wish I may, wish I might*
내가 할 수 있으면 좋겠다

*Seohae Mon Amour*

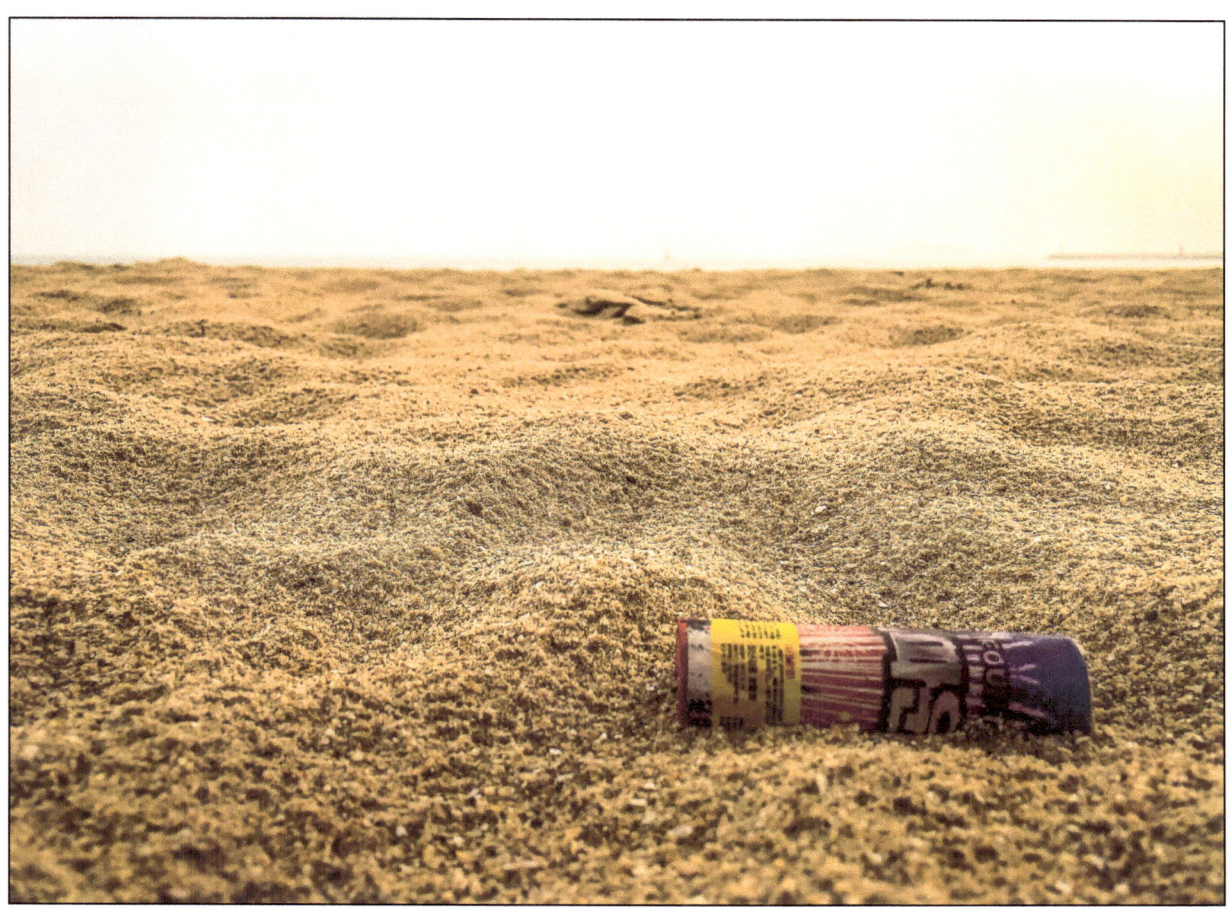

*Brass*
놋쇠

# People

Human nature sees us sometimes pursue solitude, sometimes seek friendship, and sometimes chase love. Whatever it may be someone is sure to be searching for it at *Echo Beach*. If vigilant, you may also spy couples and families sporting *couple look* (i.e., wearing the same outfits to show that they are together).

# 사람들

인간 본성은 때때로 우리가 고독을 추구하고 때로는 우정을 찾고 때로는 사랑을 좇습니다. 그것이 무엇이든, 누군가는 에코 비치에서 그것을 찾고 있을 것입니다. 주의를 기울인다면 커플룩 (즉, 똑같은 옷을 입고 함께하고 있다는 것을 보여주는)으로 입고 있는 커플 및 가족들을 볼 수도 있습니다.

*Seohae Mon Amour*

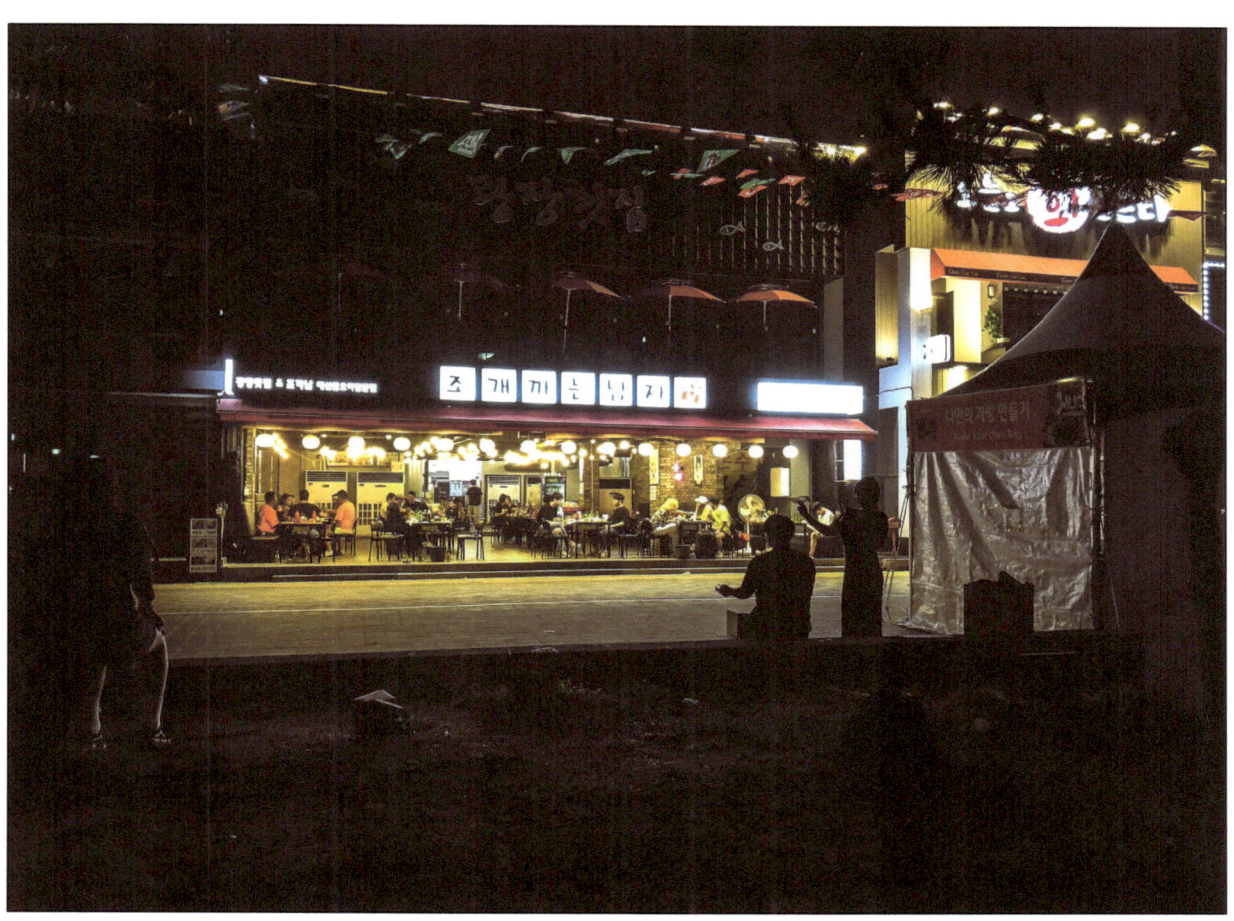

*Camelot*
평온하고 서정적인 곳

# Echo Beach

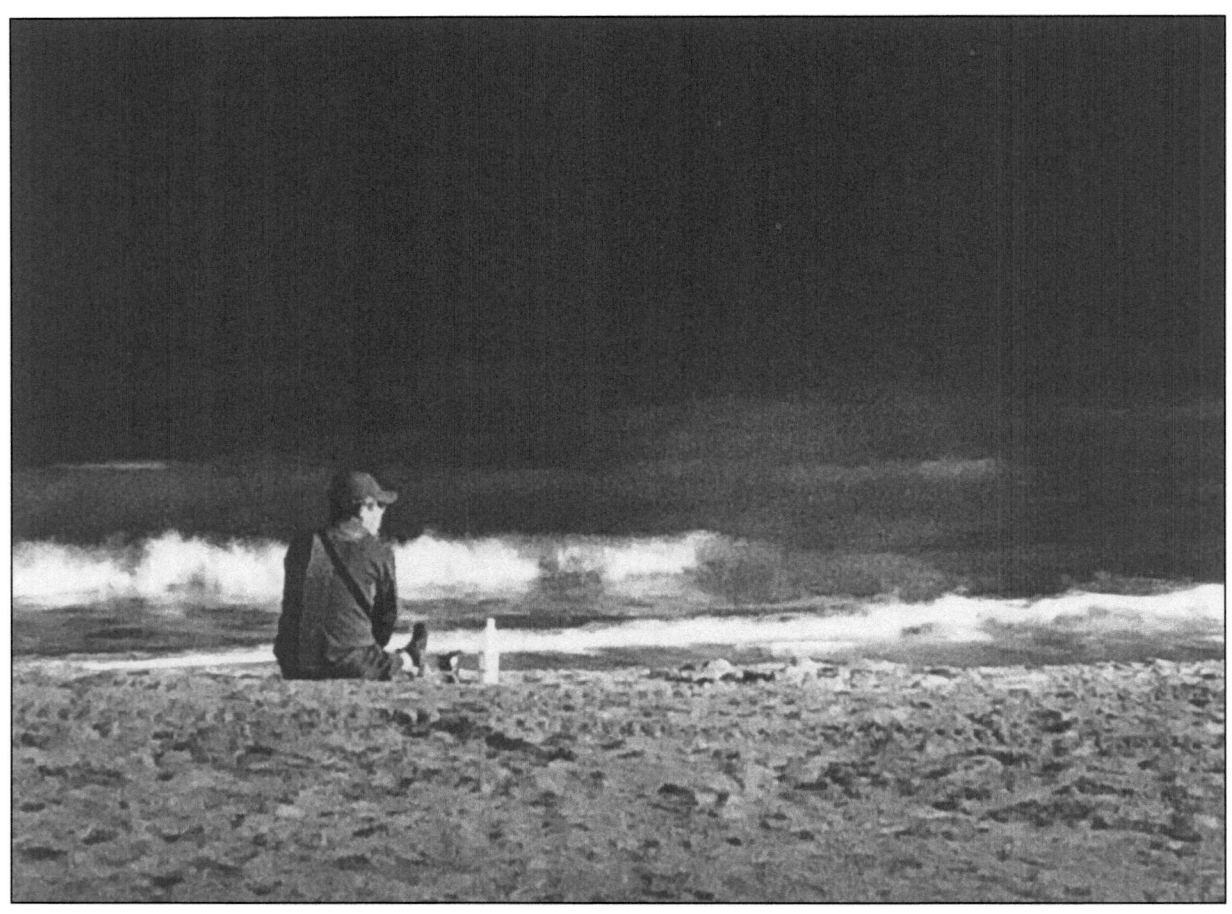

*Solitude sits*
앉아 있는 고독

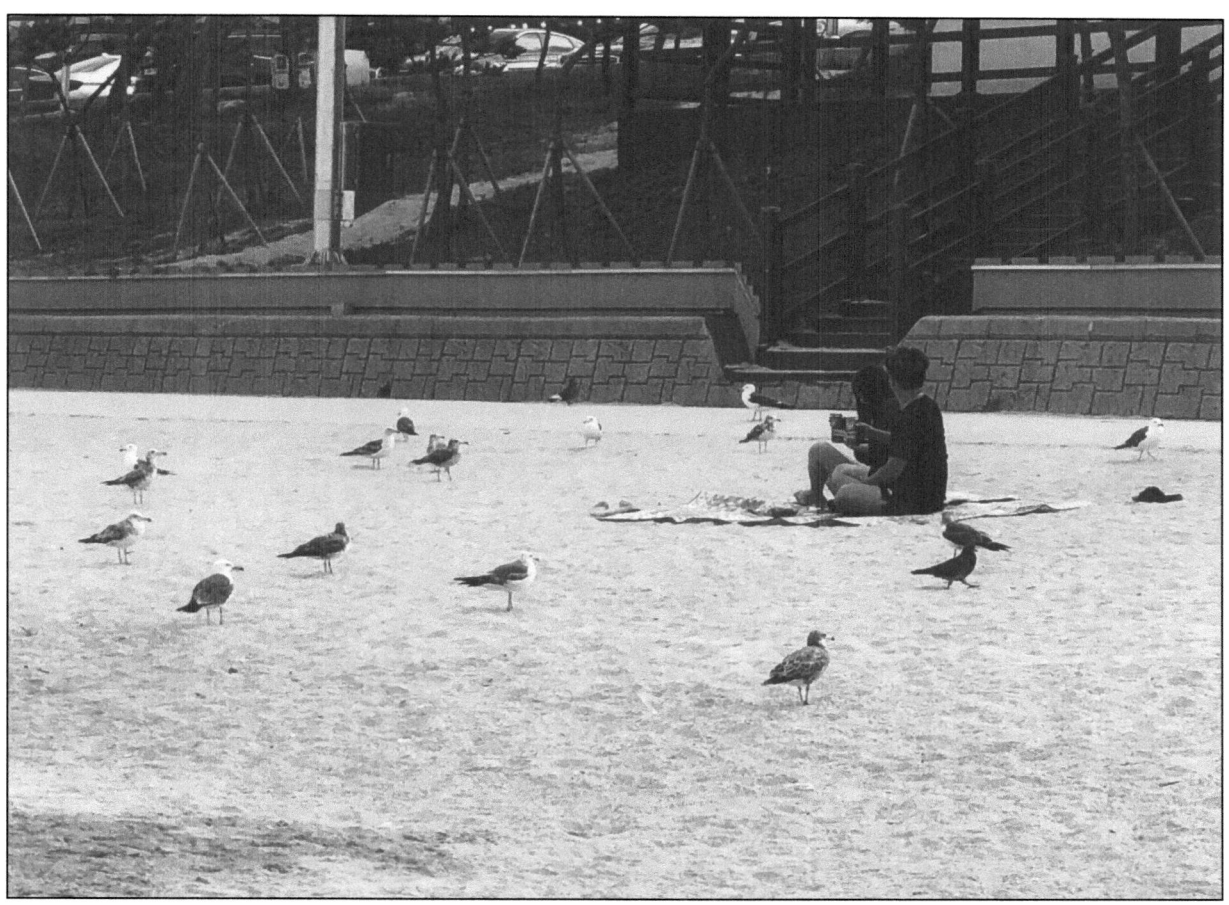

*Couple sits*
앉아 있는 커플

# Echo Beach

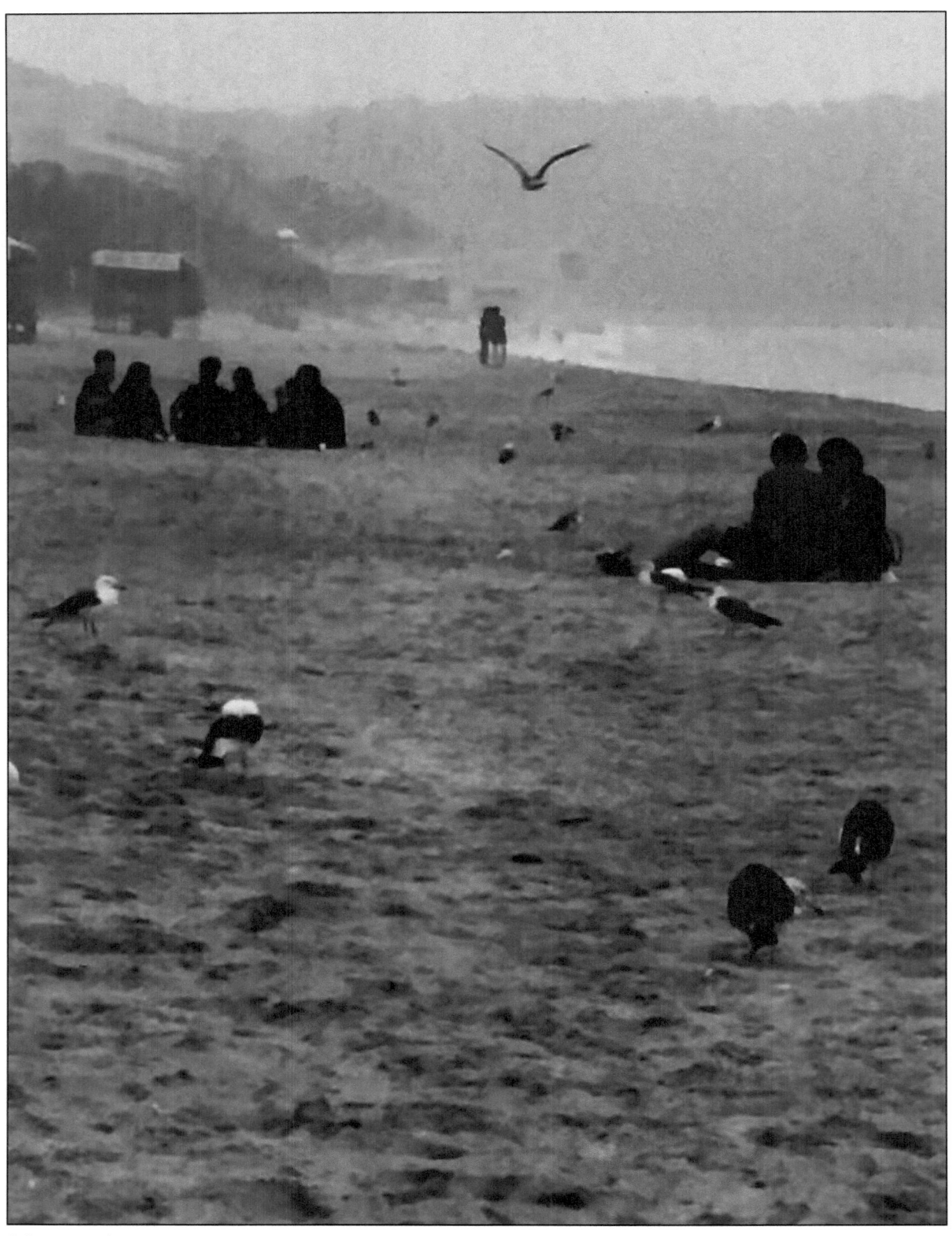

*Solitary couples*
홀로 있는 커플들

*Seohae Mon Amour*

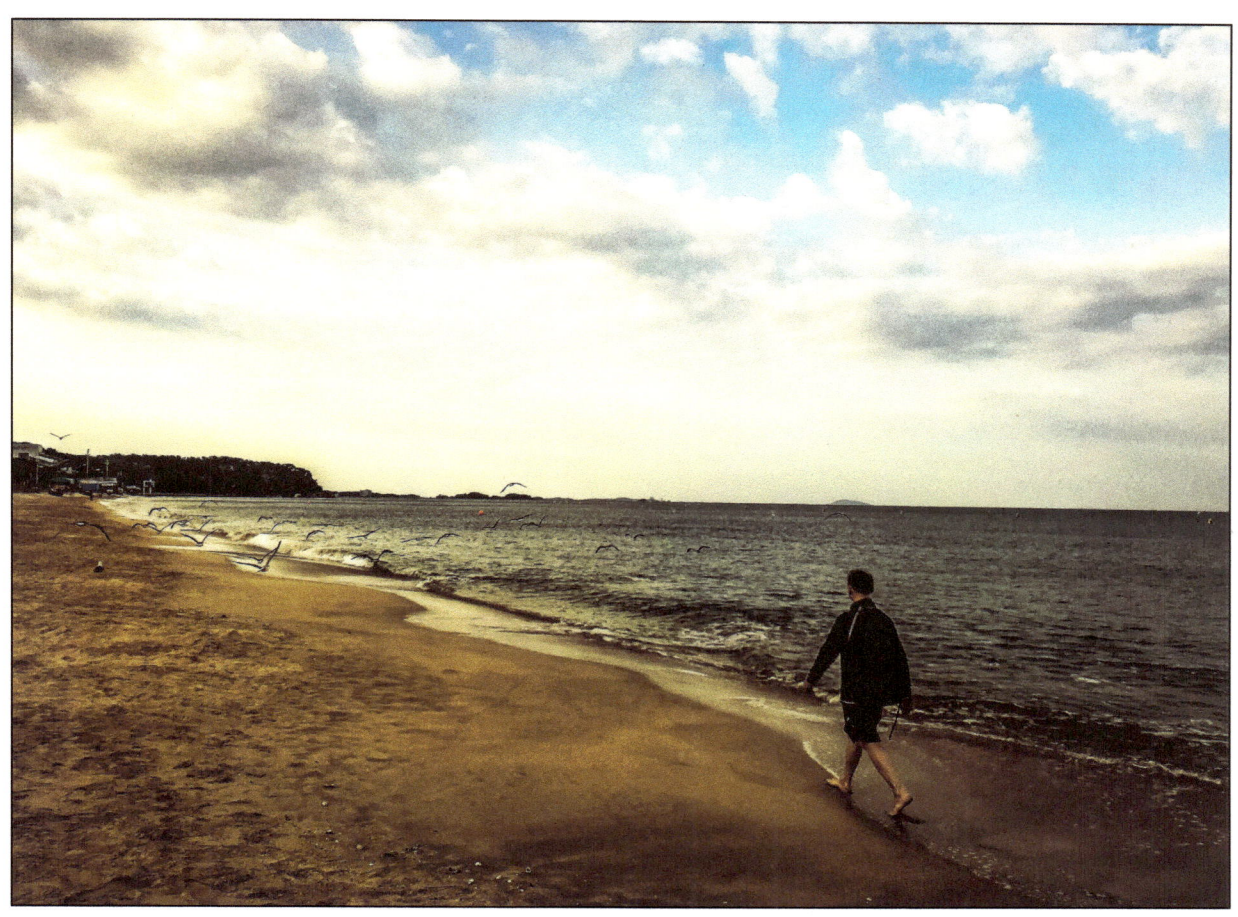

*Solitude walks*
고독의 산책

# Echo Beach

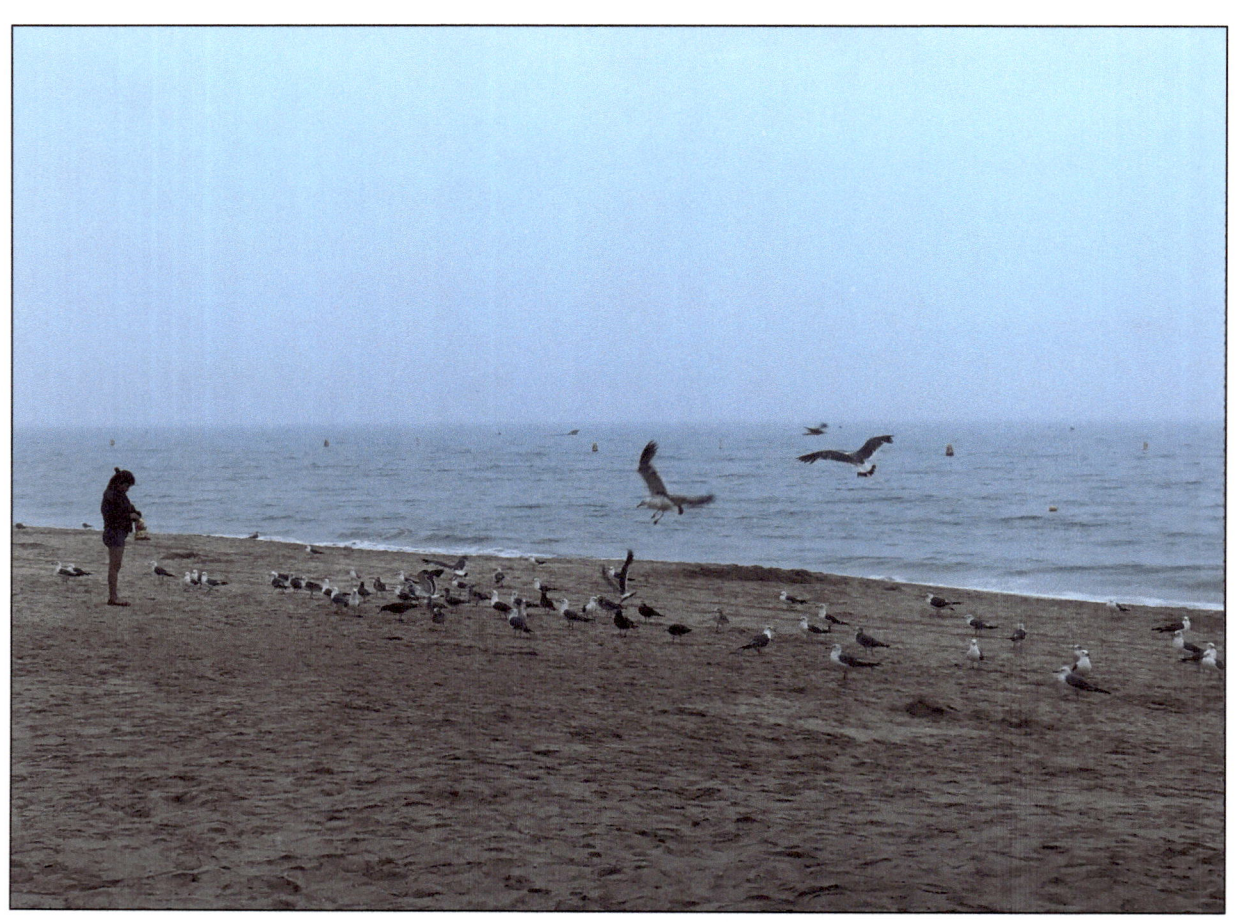

*Solitude feeds*
고독의 먹이

# Seohae Mon Amour

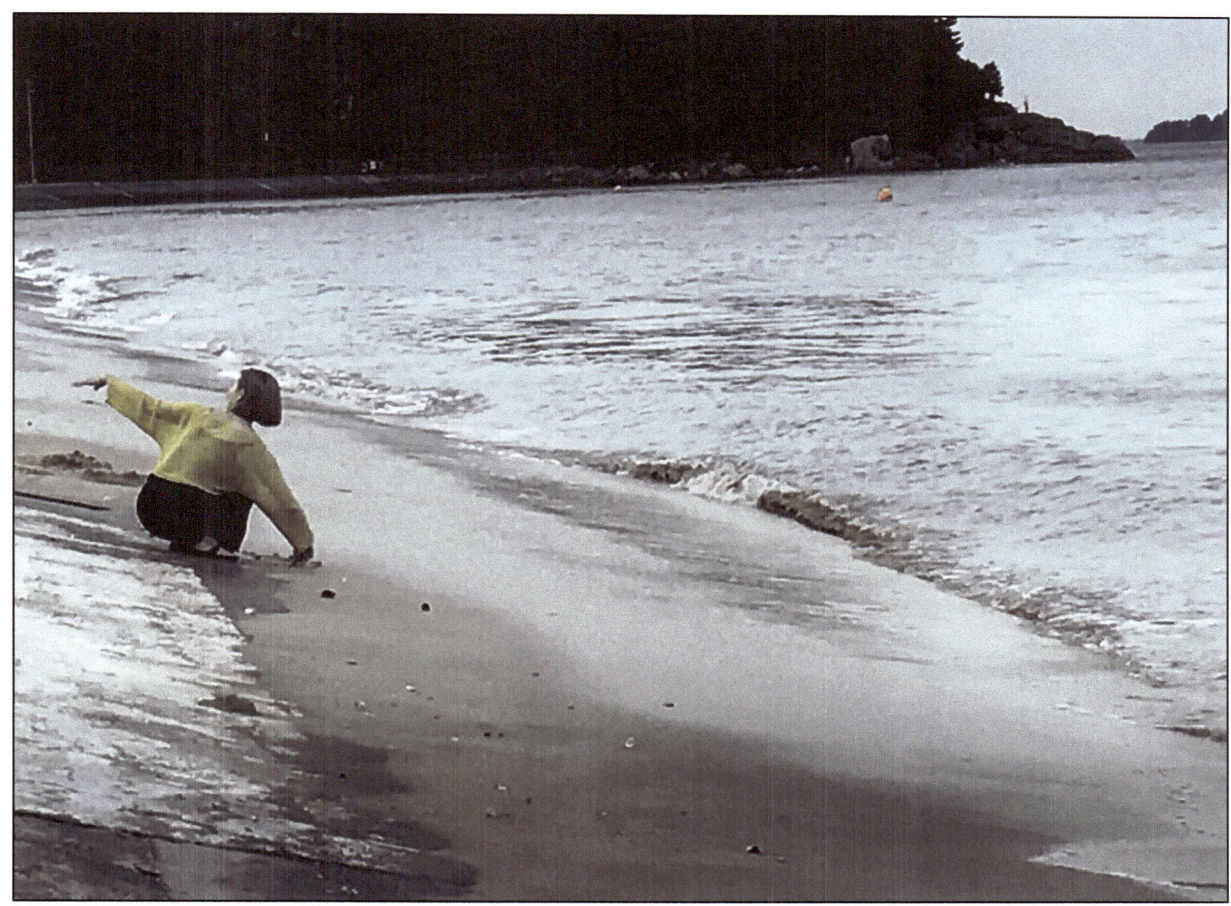

*Solitude beckons*
고독의 손짓

# Echo Beach

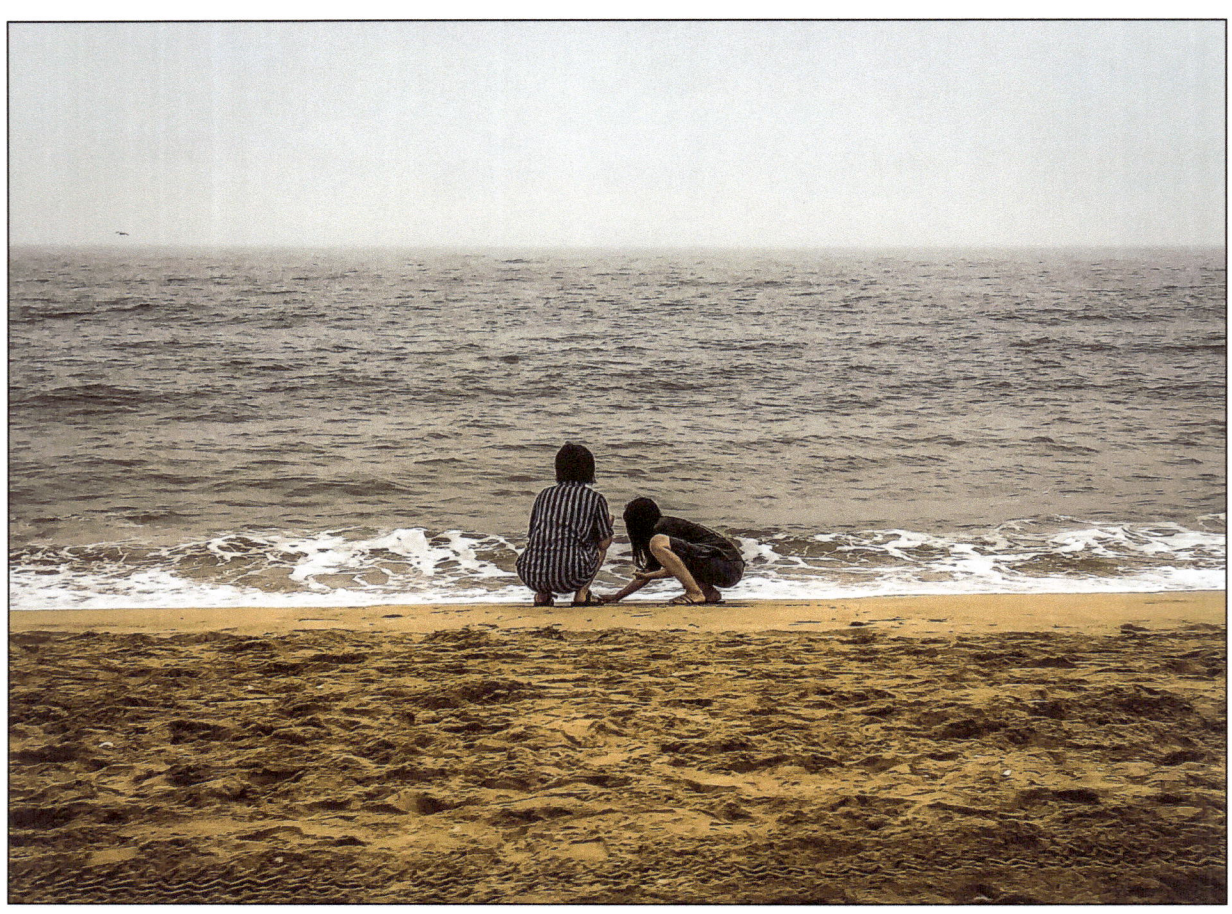

*Couple do*
노는 커플

*Seohae Mon Amour*

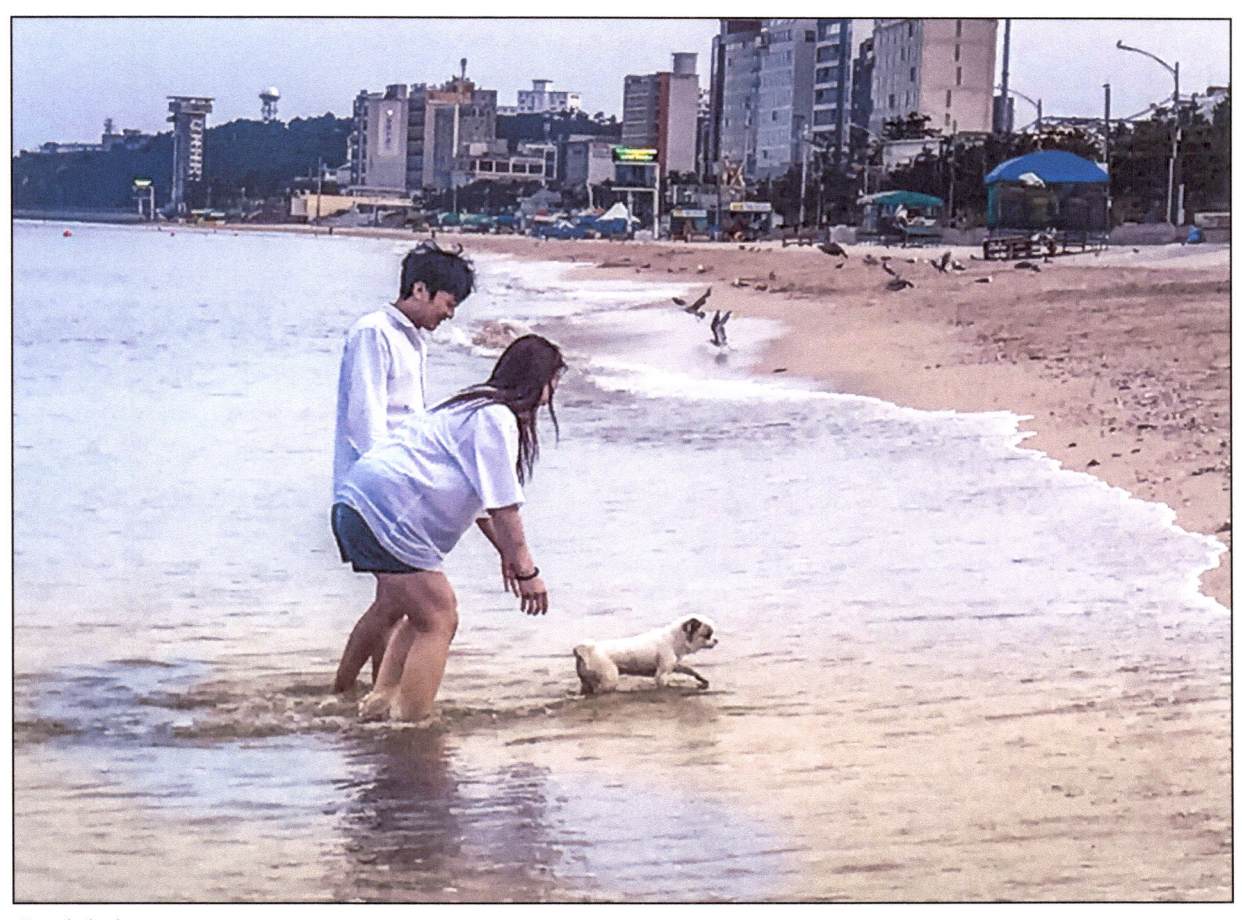

*Couple look*
바라보는 커플

# An Industry

The beaches of the west coast that are accessible are heavily urbanized. Asphalt and stores line the sands, and the industries that have migrated to its shores depend upon the sea, tourists, and the coasts dense population for their livelihood. These industries also bring with them some unique sights.

# 산업

서해안에 있는 해변은 접근성이 좋으며 심하게 도시화되 있습니다. 아스팔트와 상점들이 모래사장을 따라 줄지어 있으며, 해안으로 이동한 산업은 그들의 생계를 바다, 관광객, 해안에 밀집된 인구에 의존하고 있습니다. 이 산업은 또한 그들에게 독특한 광경을 가져다줍니다.

Seohae Mon Amour

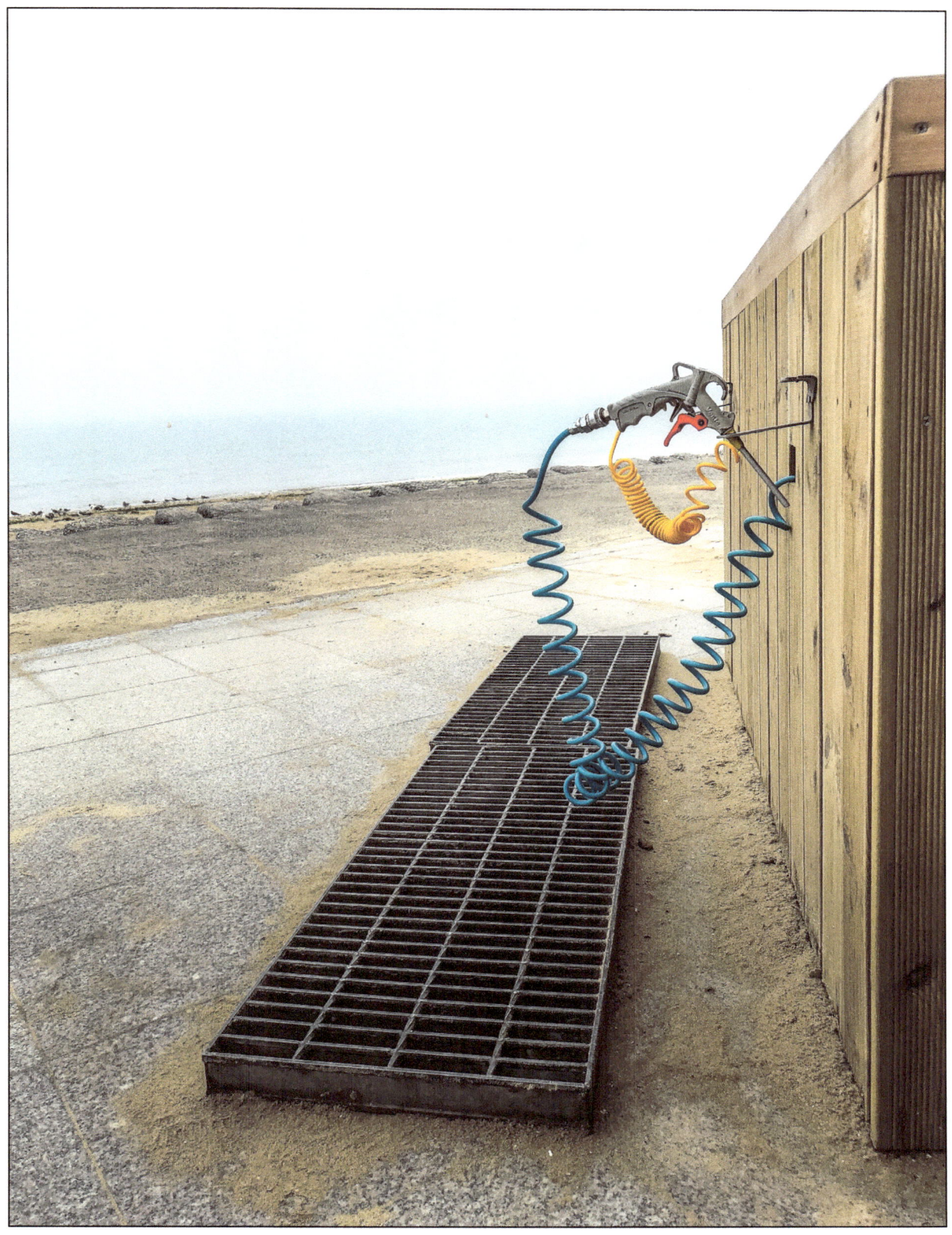

*Trigger*
트리거

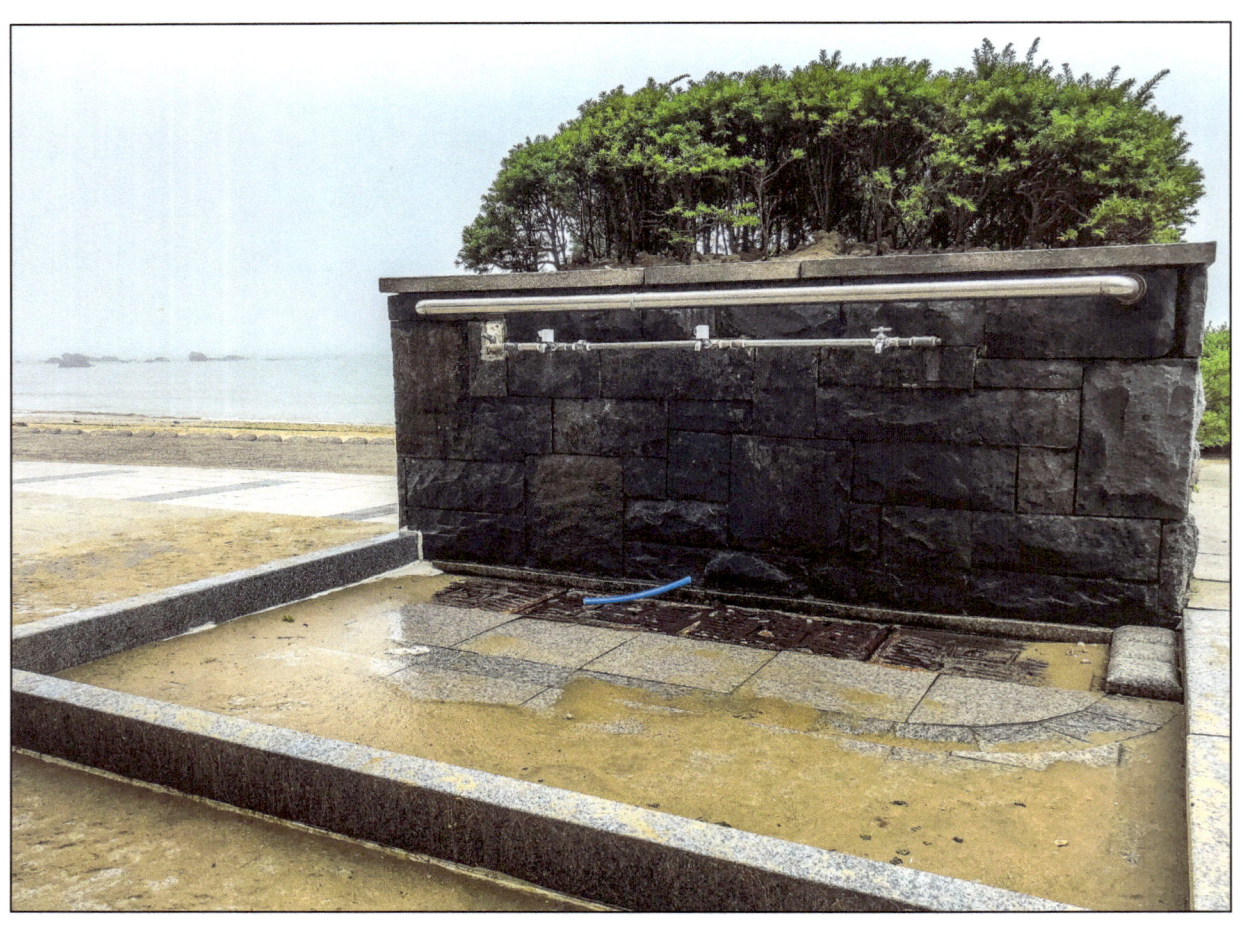

*Urban waterfalls*
도시의 폭포

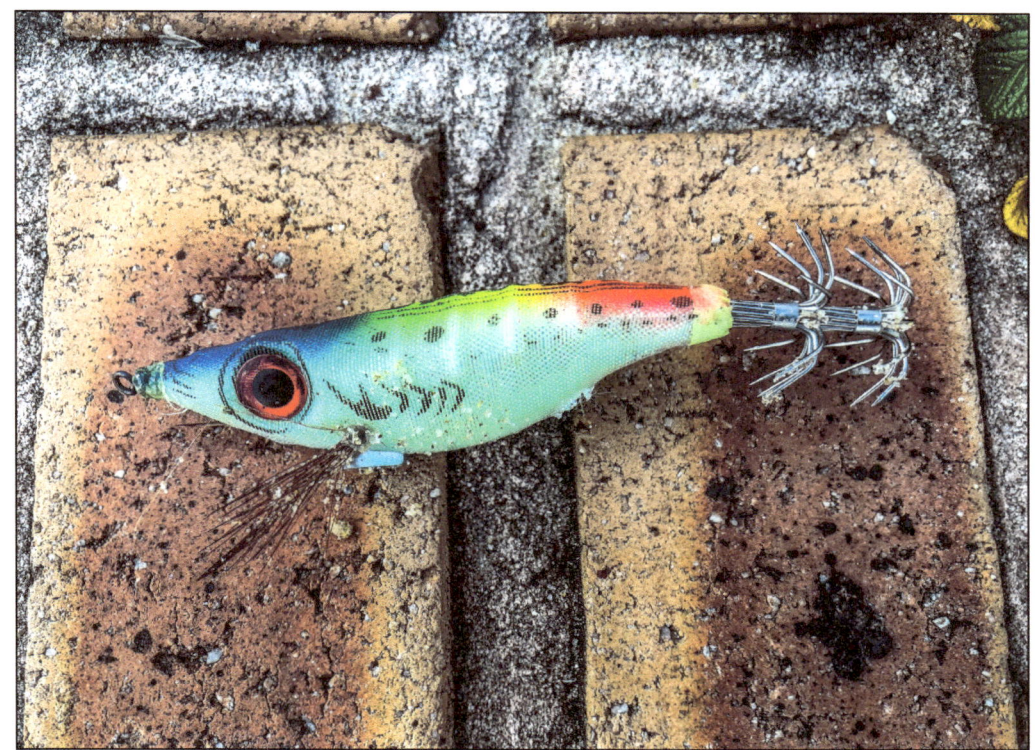

*Lure of the wild*
야생의 유혹

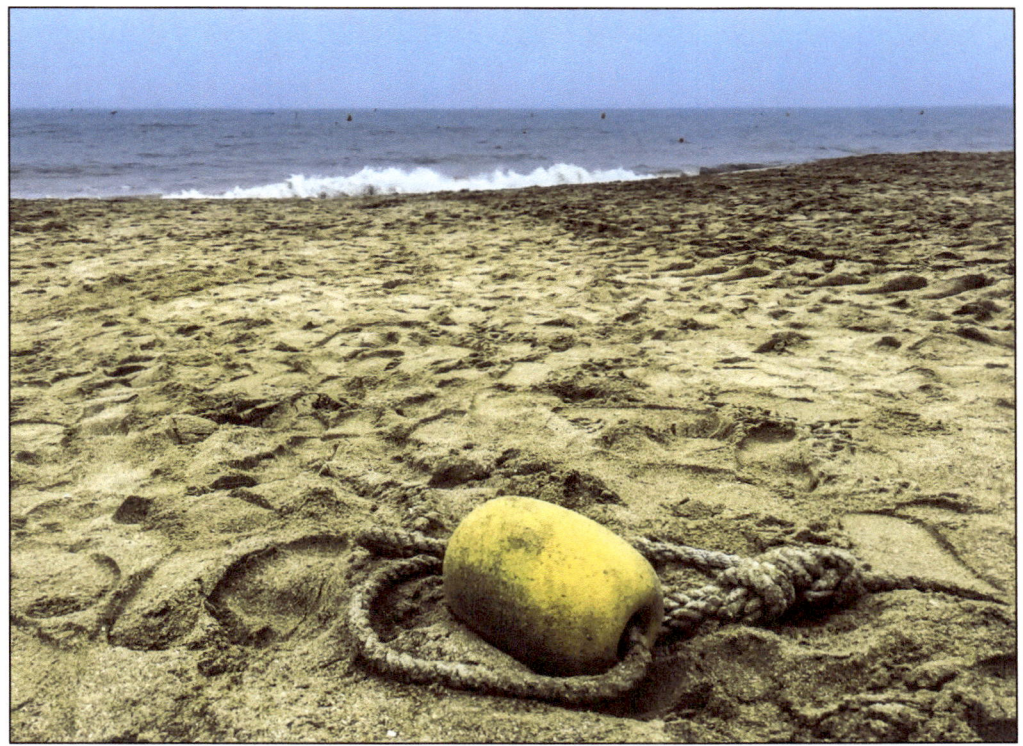

*Here, buoy!*
여기요, 부표!

# Echo Beach

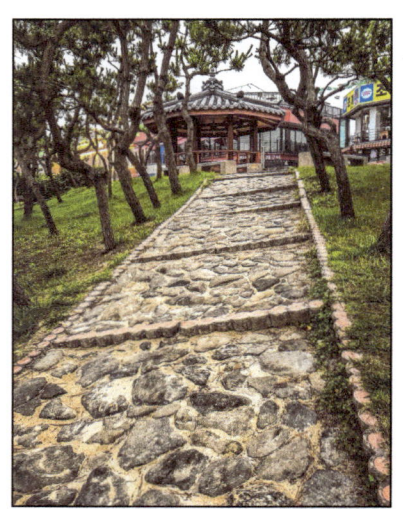 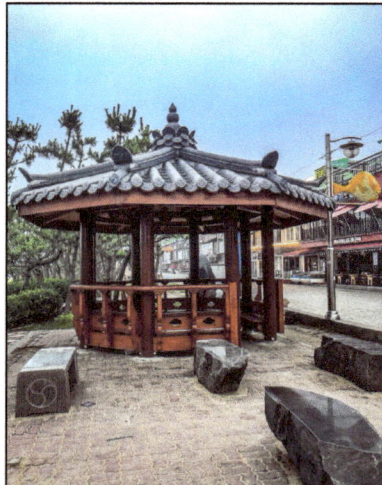 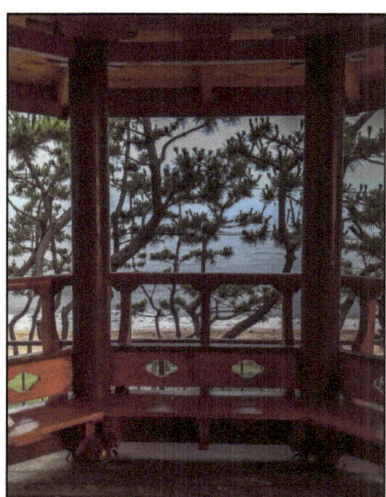

*Pagoda with a view*
전경이 내다보이는 탑

*Seohae Mon Amour*

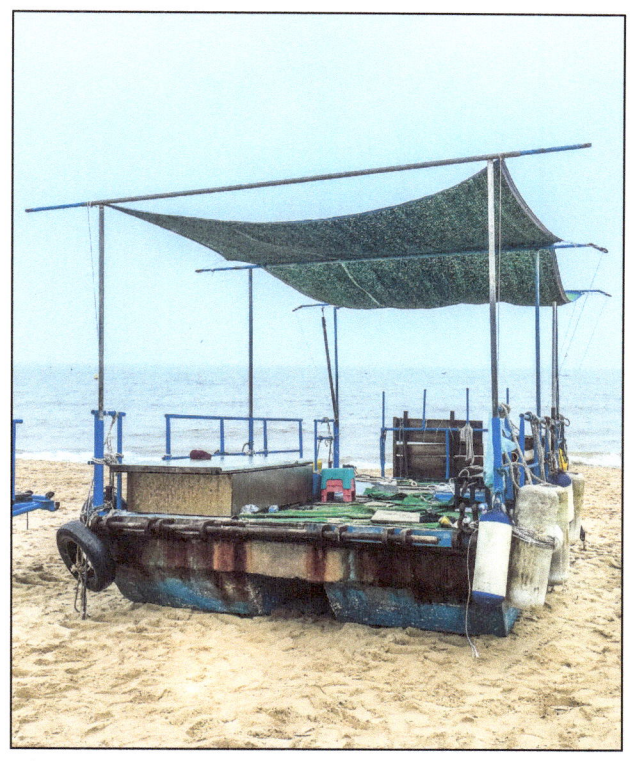

*3-hour tour*
3 시간 투어

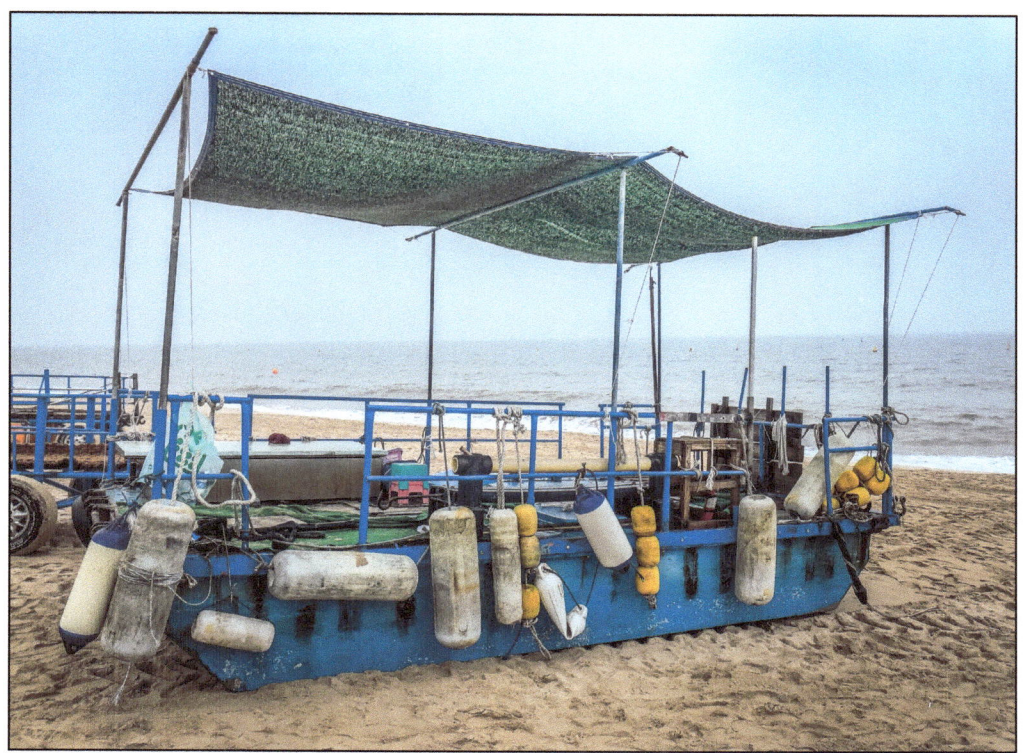

*S. S. Minnow*
에스. 에스. 미노

# Echo Beach

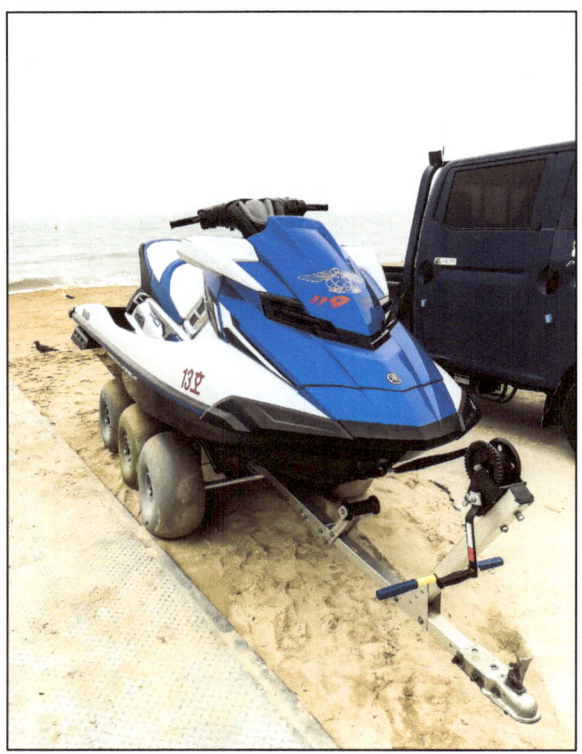

*Rescue 13*
13 호 구조

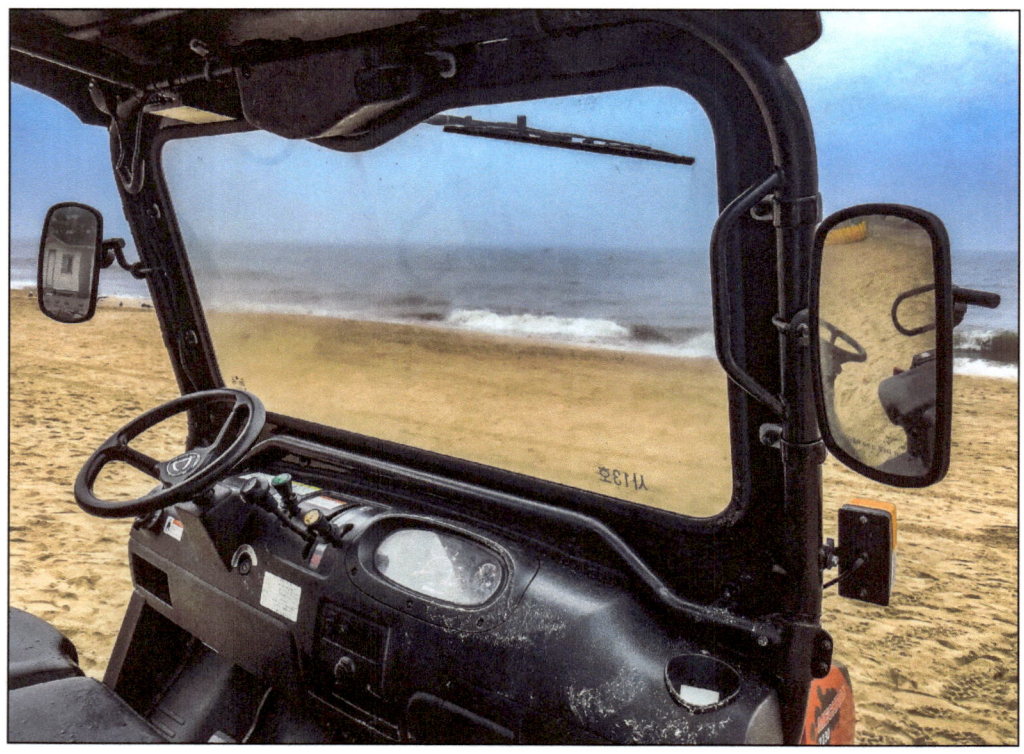

*Baywatch*
SOS 해상 구조대

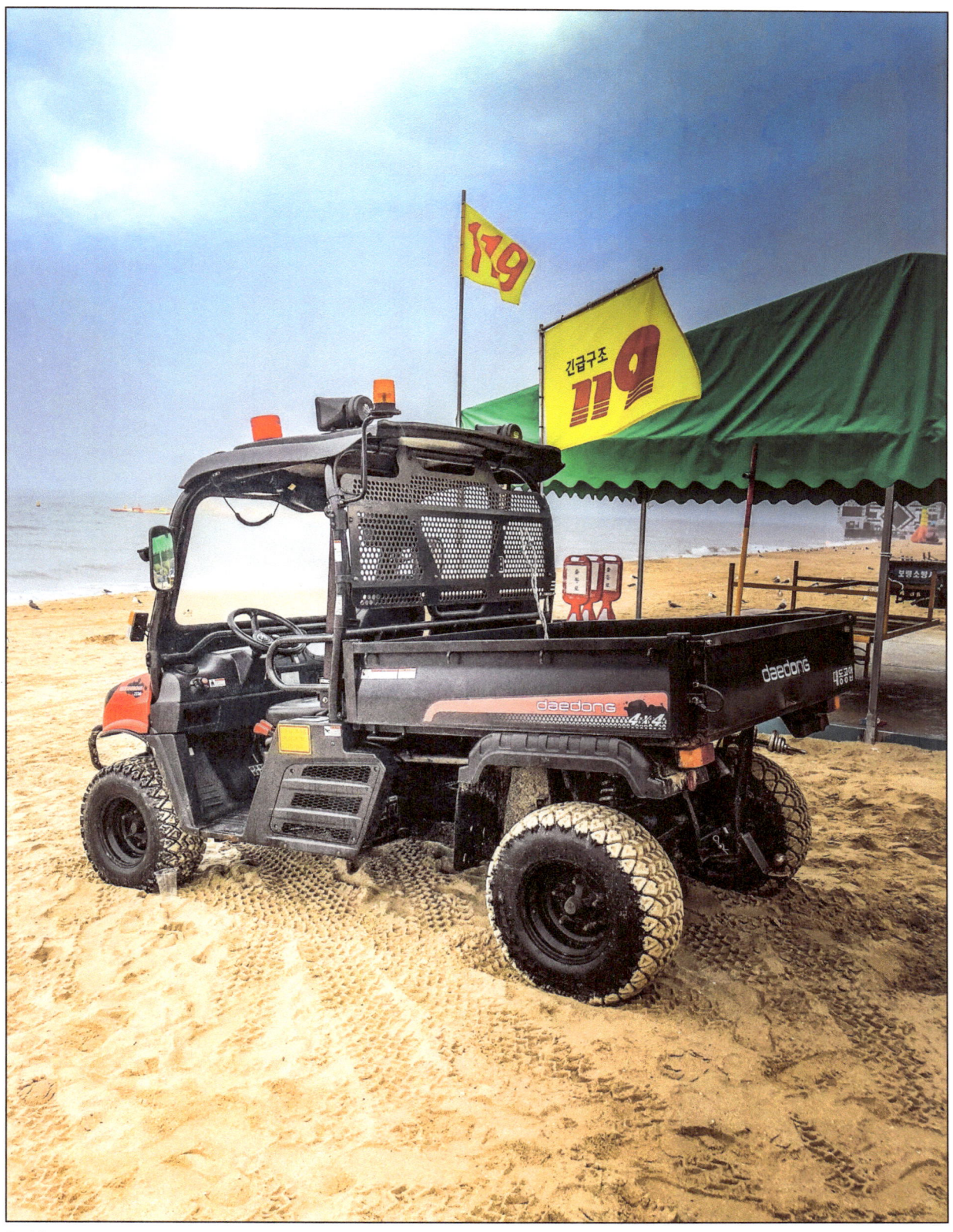

*Paddy wagon 119*
119 긴급 호송차

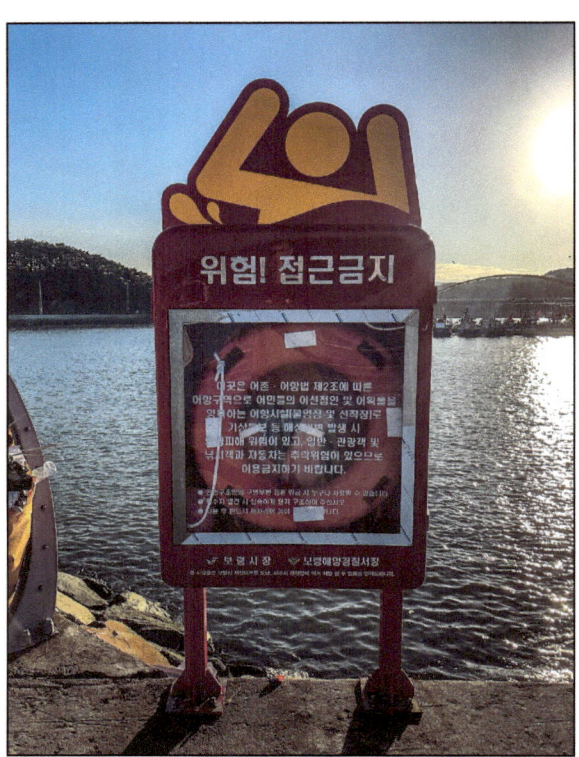

*Lifesaver*
생명의 은인

*Seohae Mon Amour*

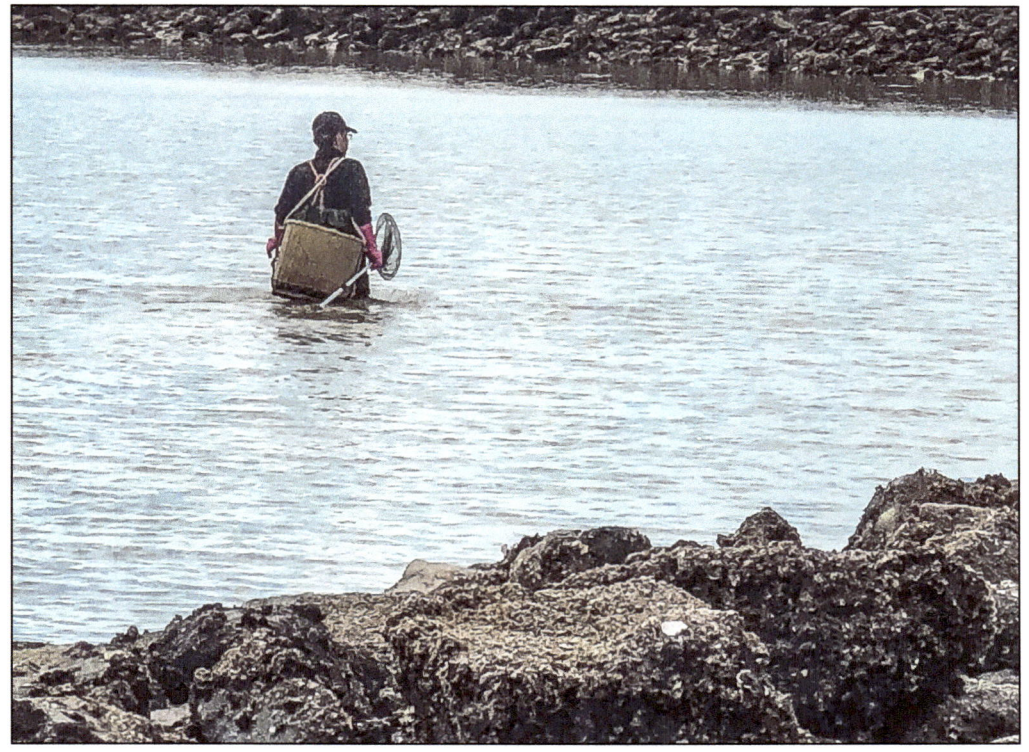

*Solitary man*
고독한 남자

# Echo Beach

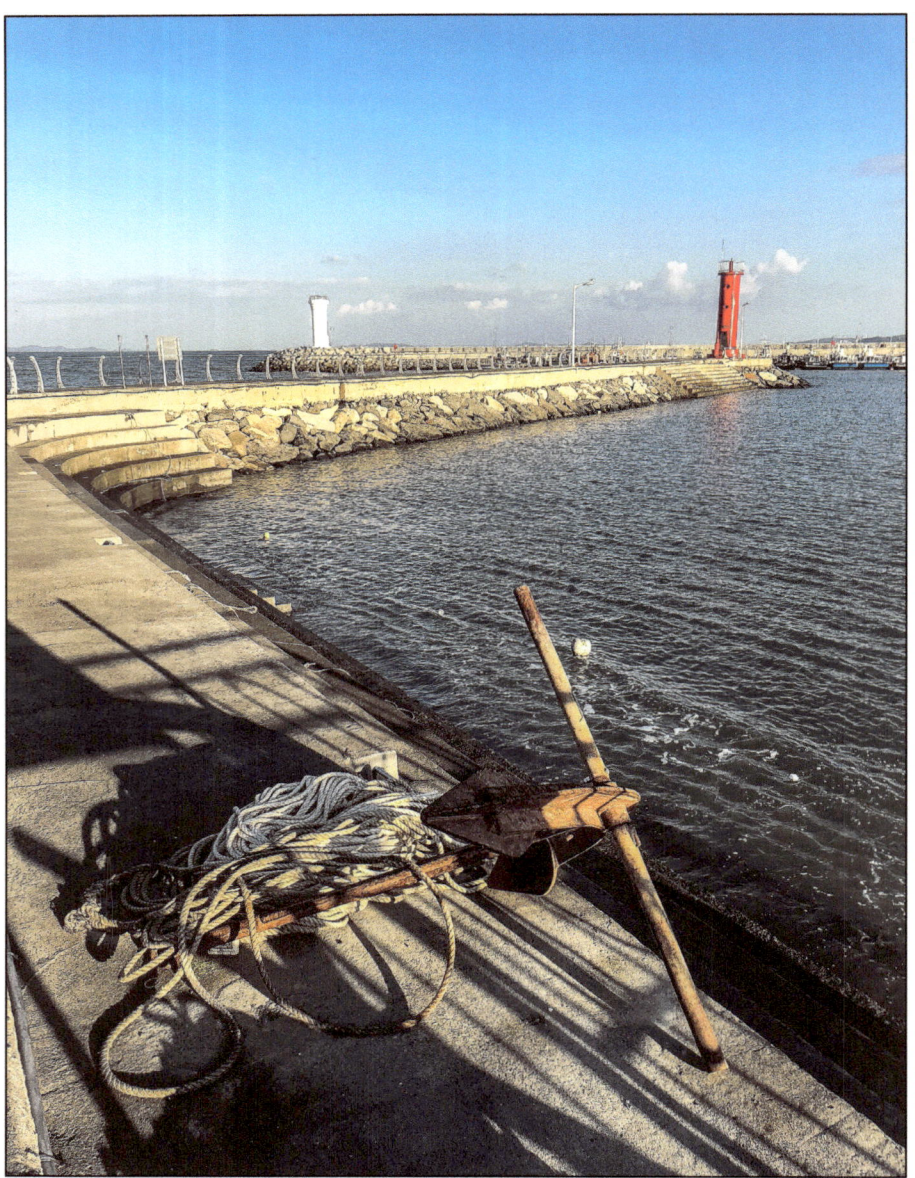

*Dead weight*
재화 중량

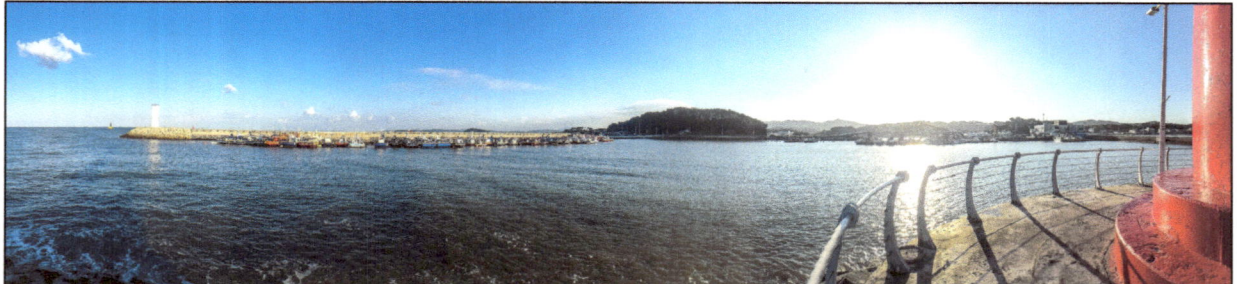

*Safe harbor*
피난항

Seohae Mon Amour

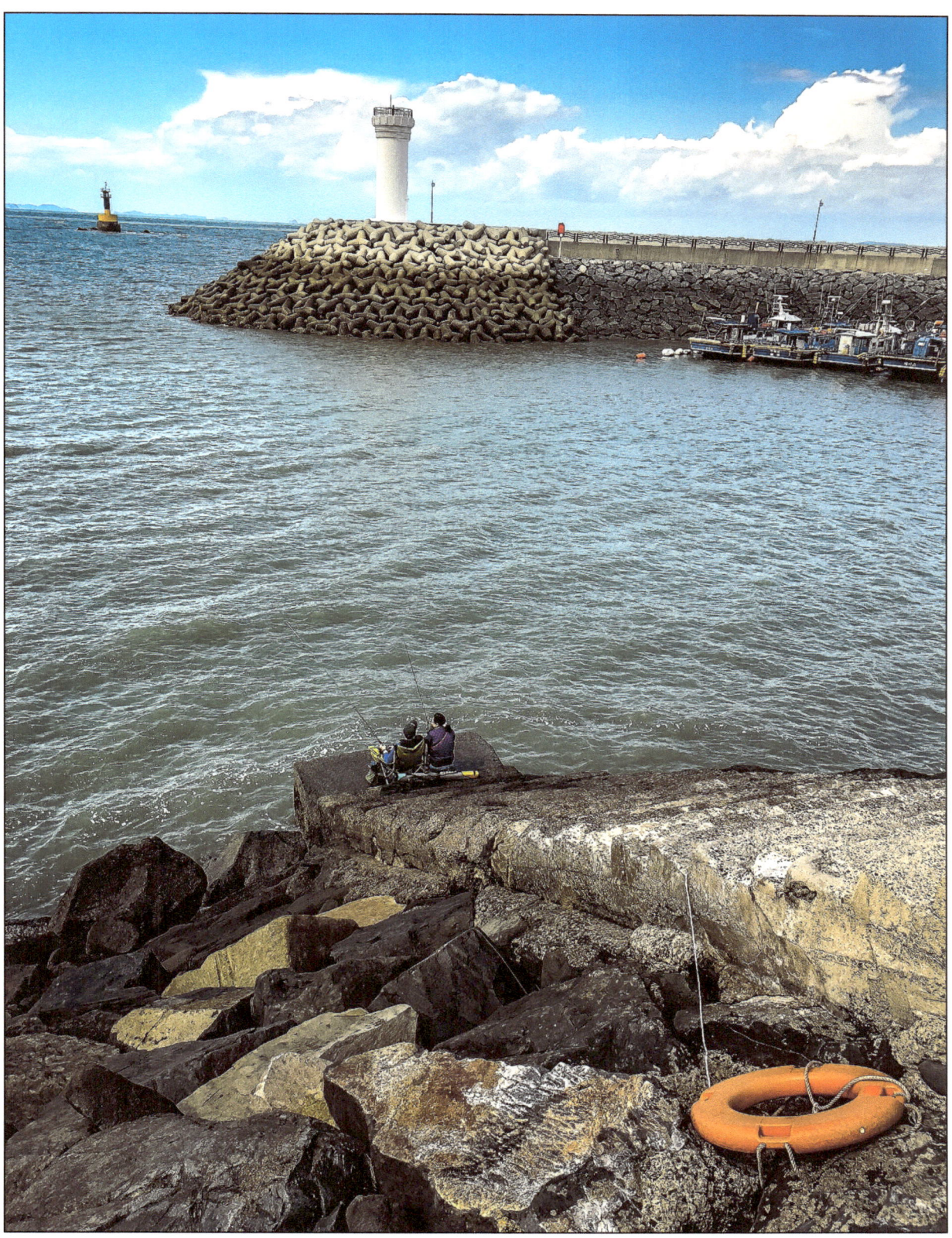

*Water's edge*
물가

Echo Beach

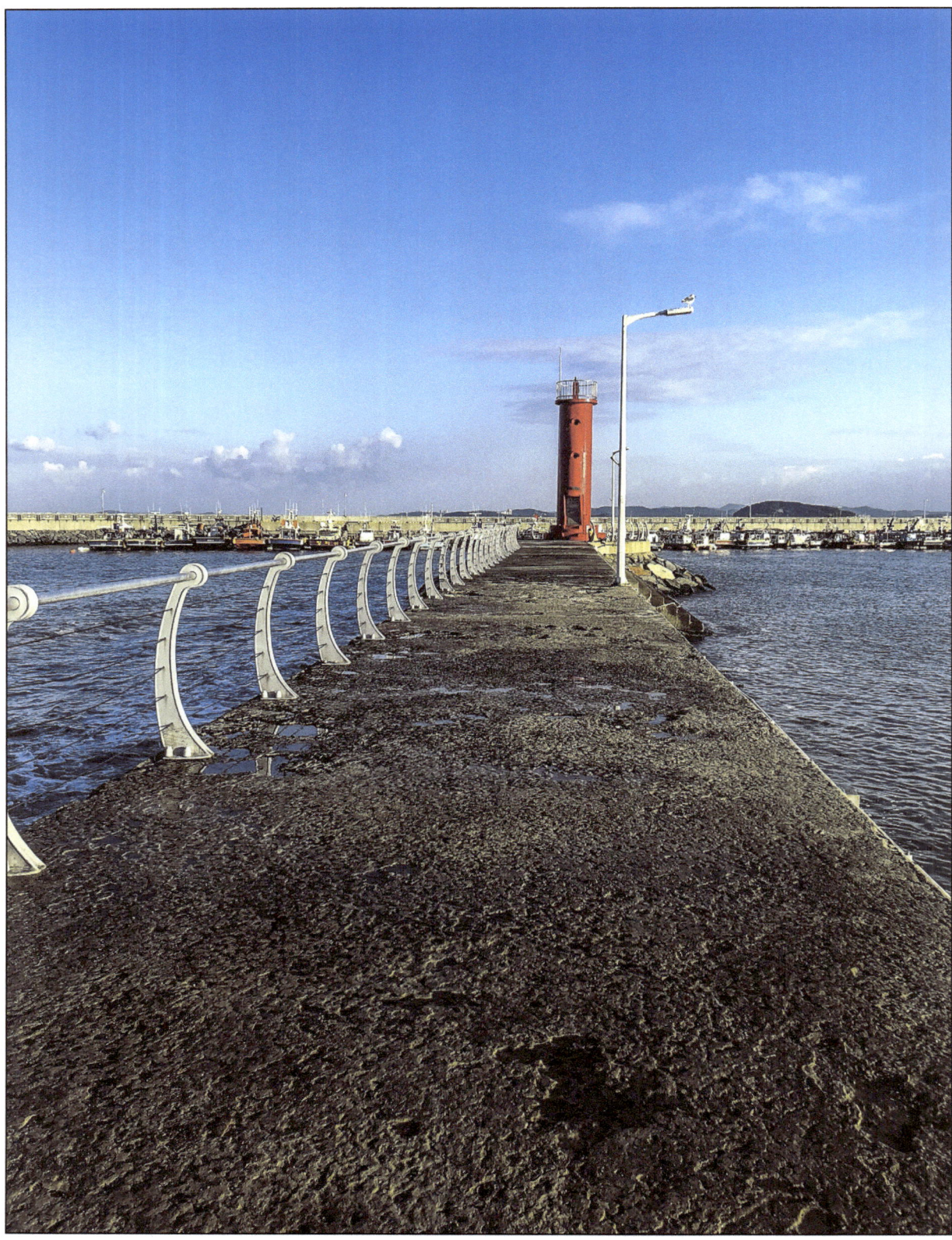

*Pier's end*
부두 끝

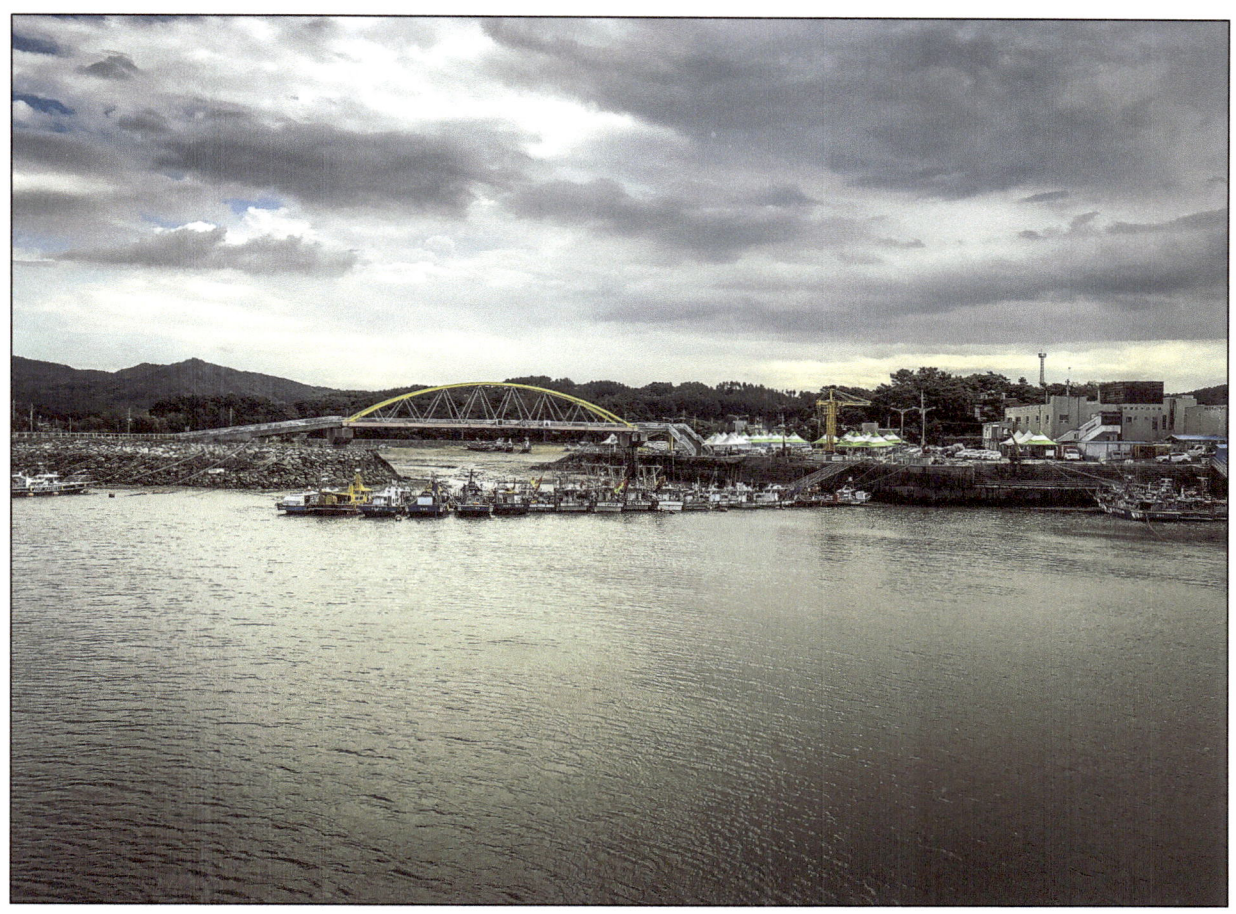

*Throw a shrimp in yellow wine*
새우를 노란 포도주에 던지다

# Tourist Traps

Bars, karaoke rooms, restaurants, games, and rides abound year-round along the shores of the western coast. As fishermen catch fish, lobsters, and other seafood in their traps, eager entrepreneurs seek to entice tourists with the glitz and glamor of discounts, specials, novelties, trinkets, souvenirs, and special events. Perhaps two of the most famous west coast annual events today are the Boryeong Mud Festival and the Jindo Miracle Sea Road Festival.

# 관광객 덫

서해안의 해변가를 따라 일 년 내내 술집, 노래방, 레스토랑, 게임 및 놀이기구가 많이 있습니다. 어부가 물고기, 바닷가재 및 기타 해산물을 덫으로 잡듯이 열성적인 상인은 할인, 특별상품, 장식품, 장신구, 기념품 및 특별 행사라는 현란함과 화려함으로 관광객을 유인하려 합니다. 아마도 서해안의 가장 유명한 연례행사 두 개는 '보령 머드 축제'와 '진도 신비의 바닷길 축제'입니다.

*Seohae Mon Amour*

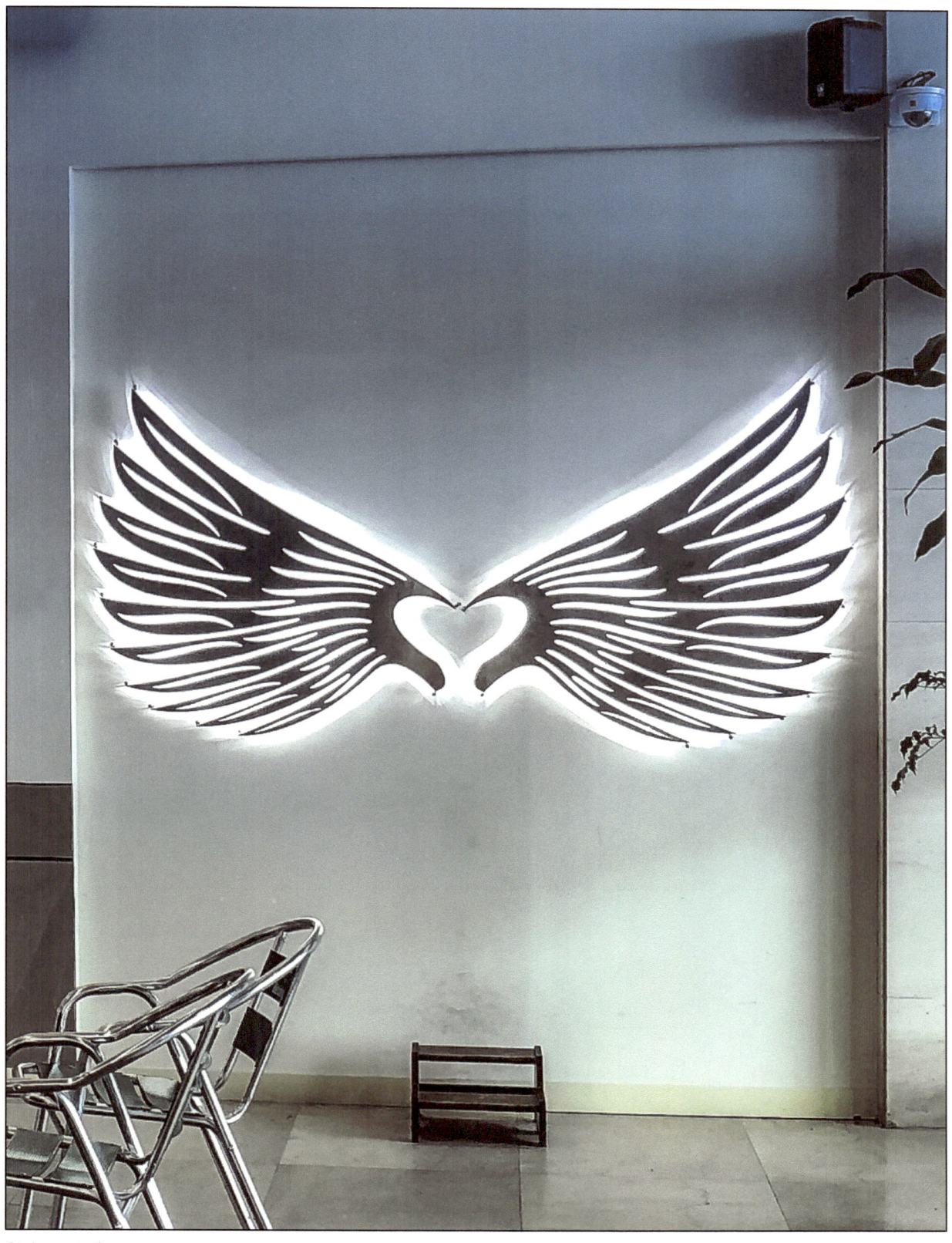

*Stairway to heaven*
천국의 계단

Echo Beach

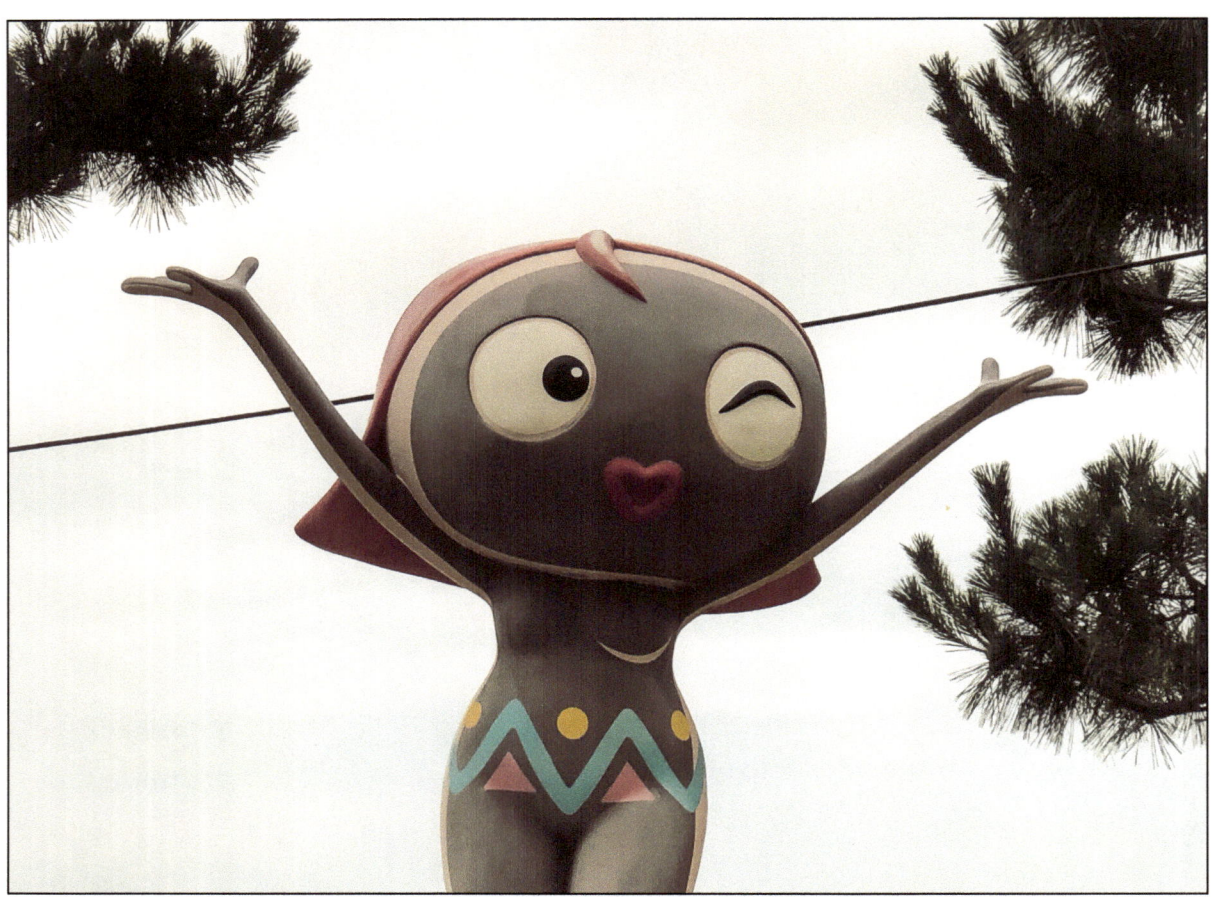

*Mud girl*
진흙 소녀

# Seohae Mon Amour

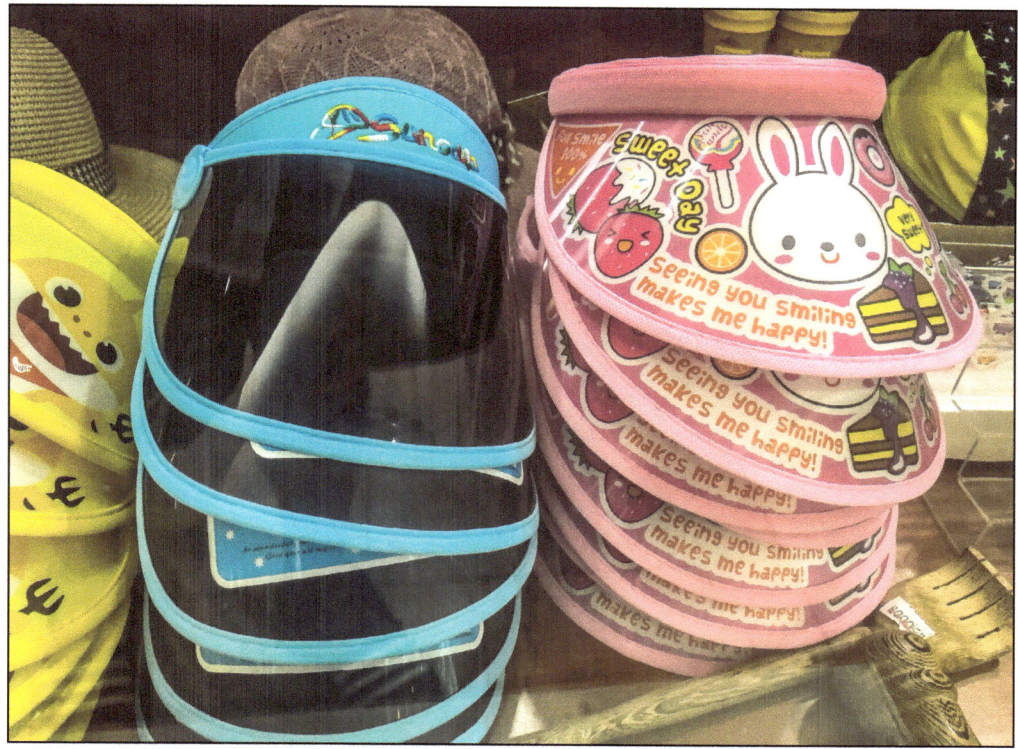

*I'm melting*
나는 녹고 있다

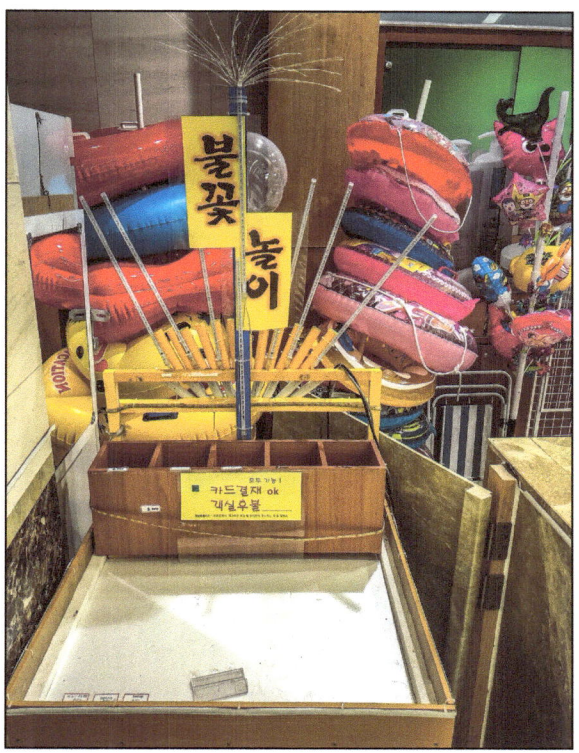

*Sold out*
매진

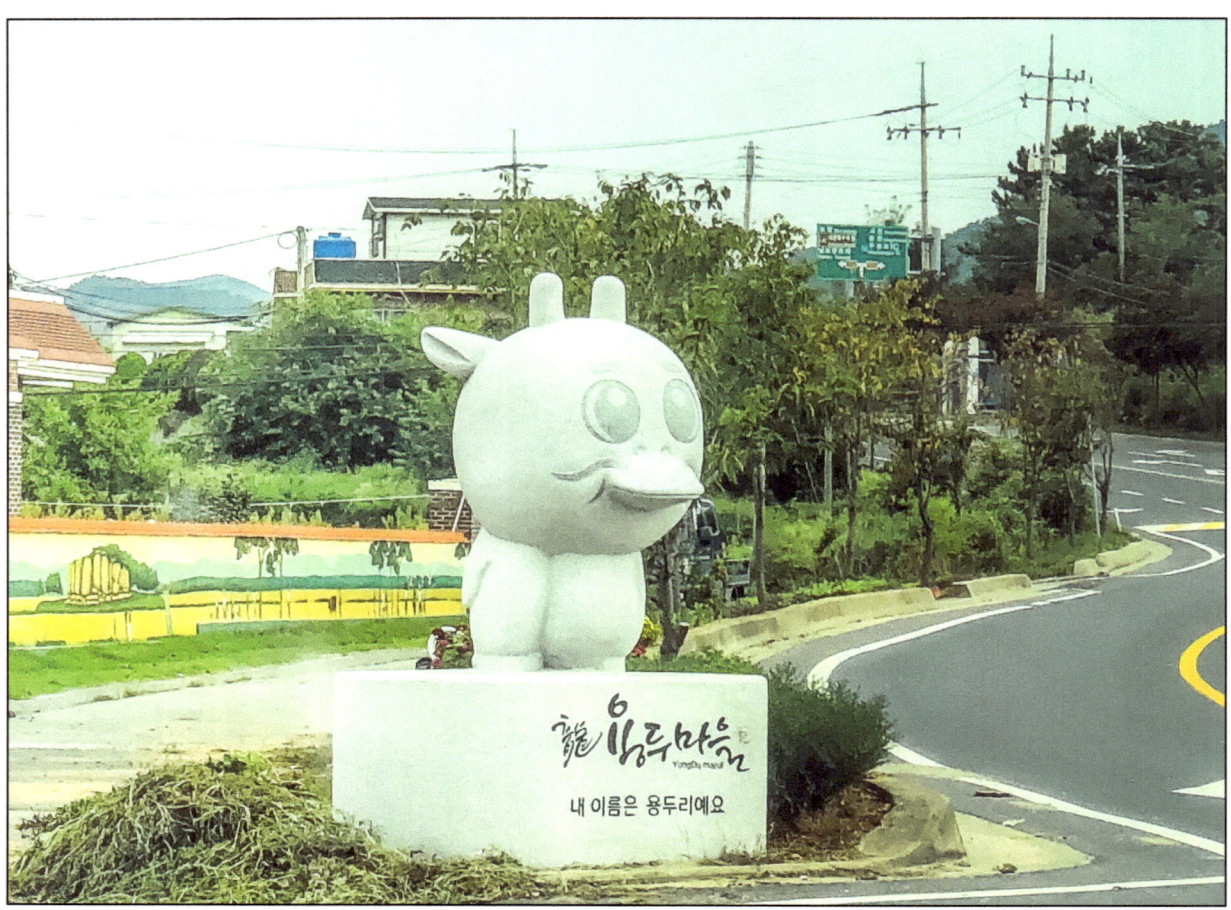

*Beach mascot 1*
비치 마스코트 1

Seohae Mon Amour

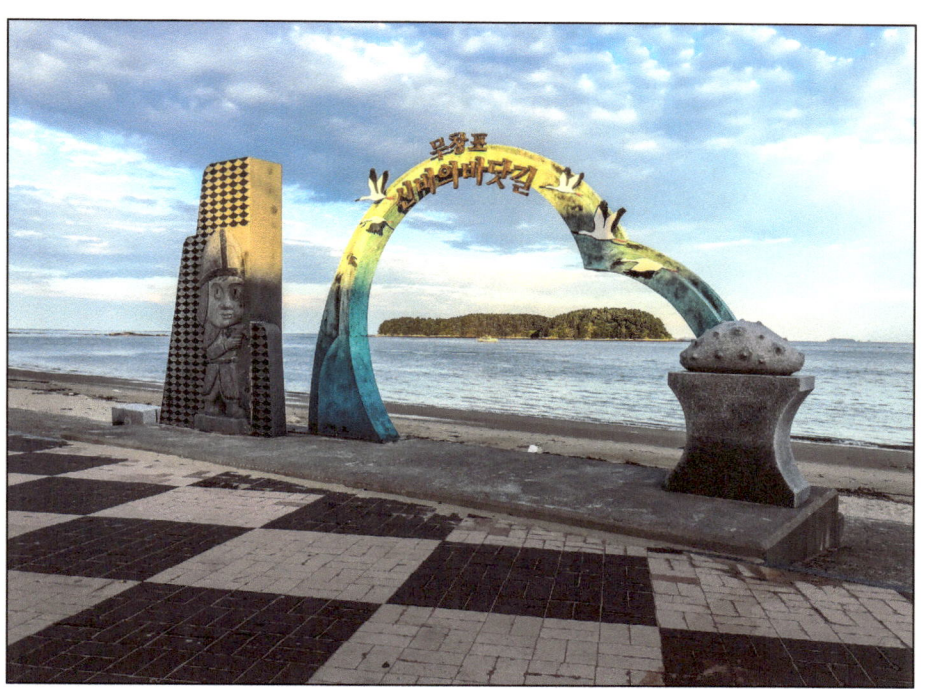

*Golden arches*
황금빛 아치들

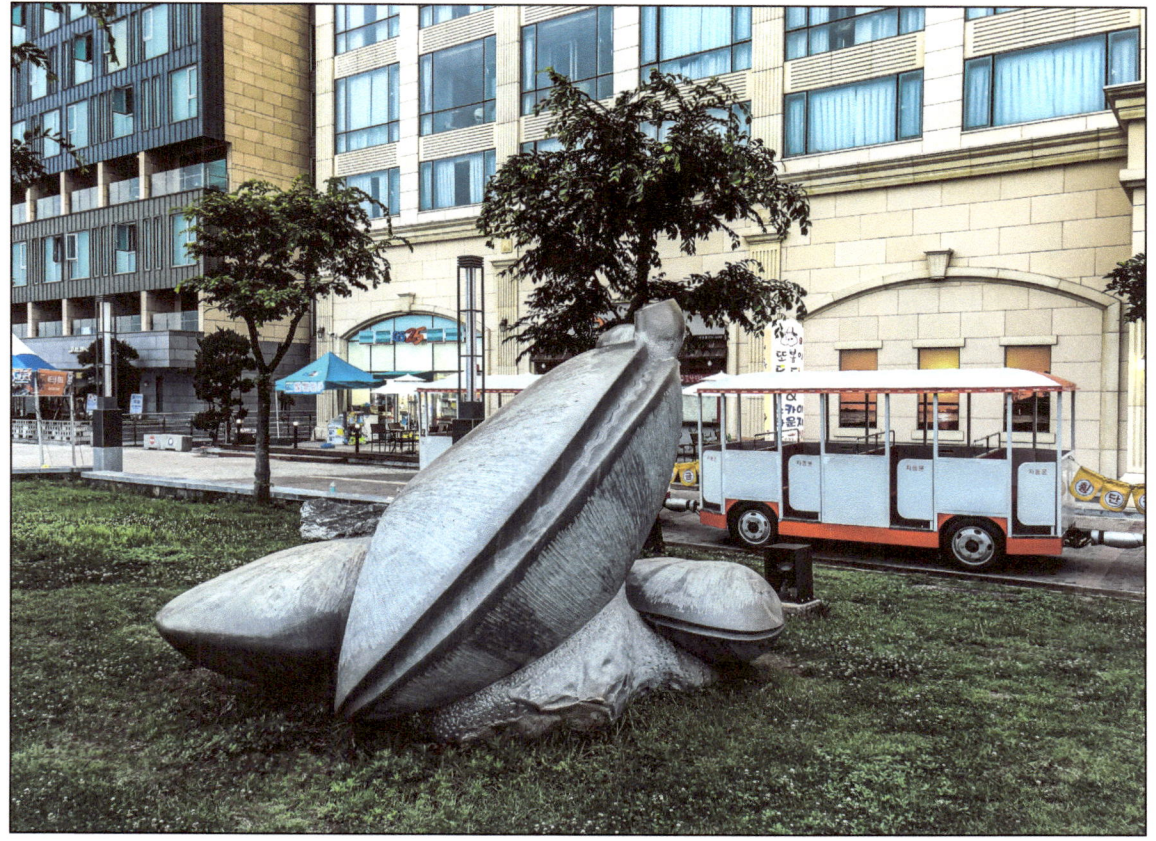

*GS25, soft-shell clam and tram*
GS25, 껍질이 연한 조개와 전차

# Echo Beach

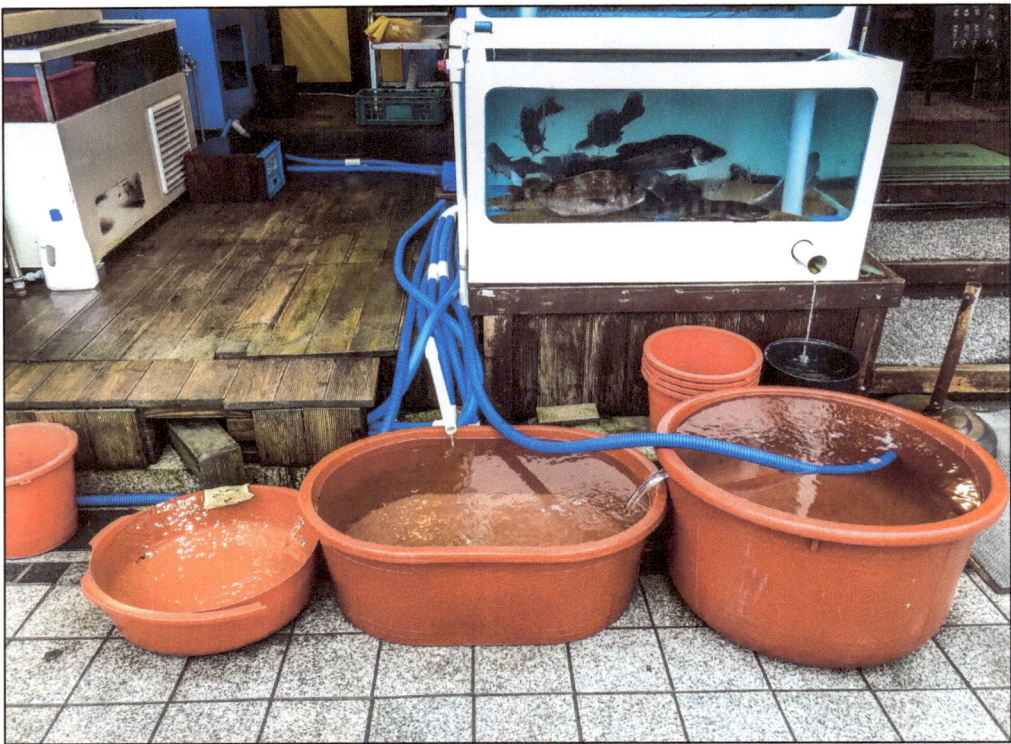

*Plastic pools*
플라스틱 대야 수영장

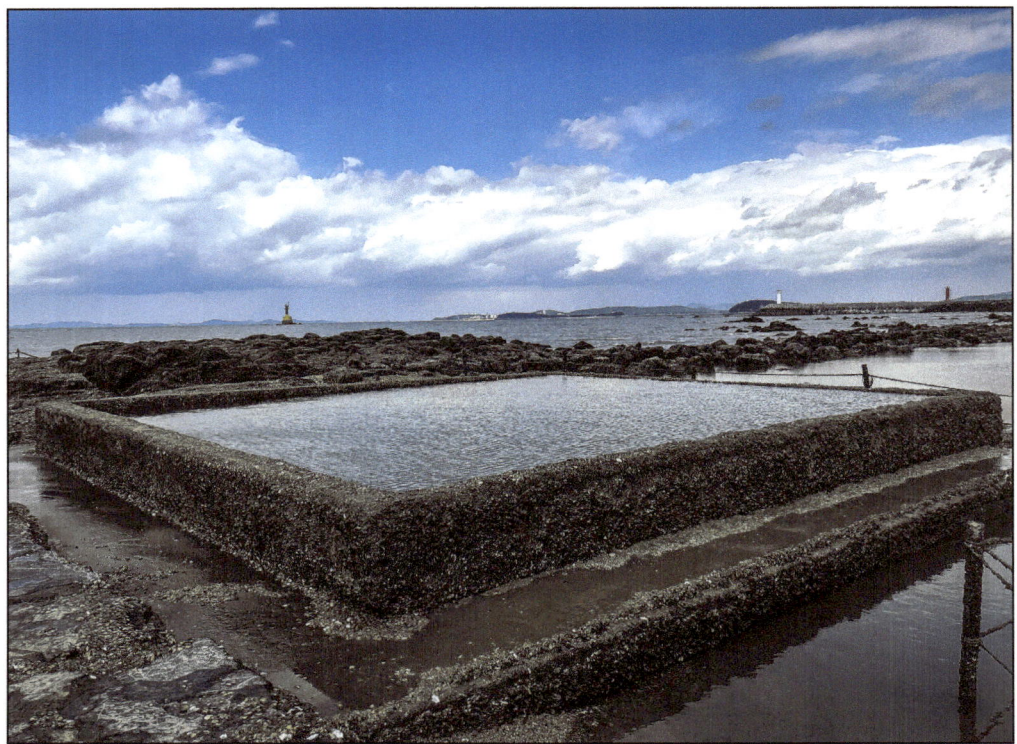

*Tidal pools*
조수 웅덩이

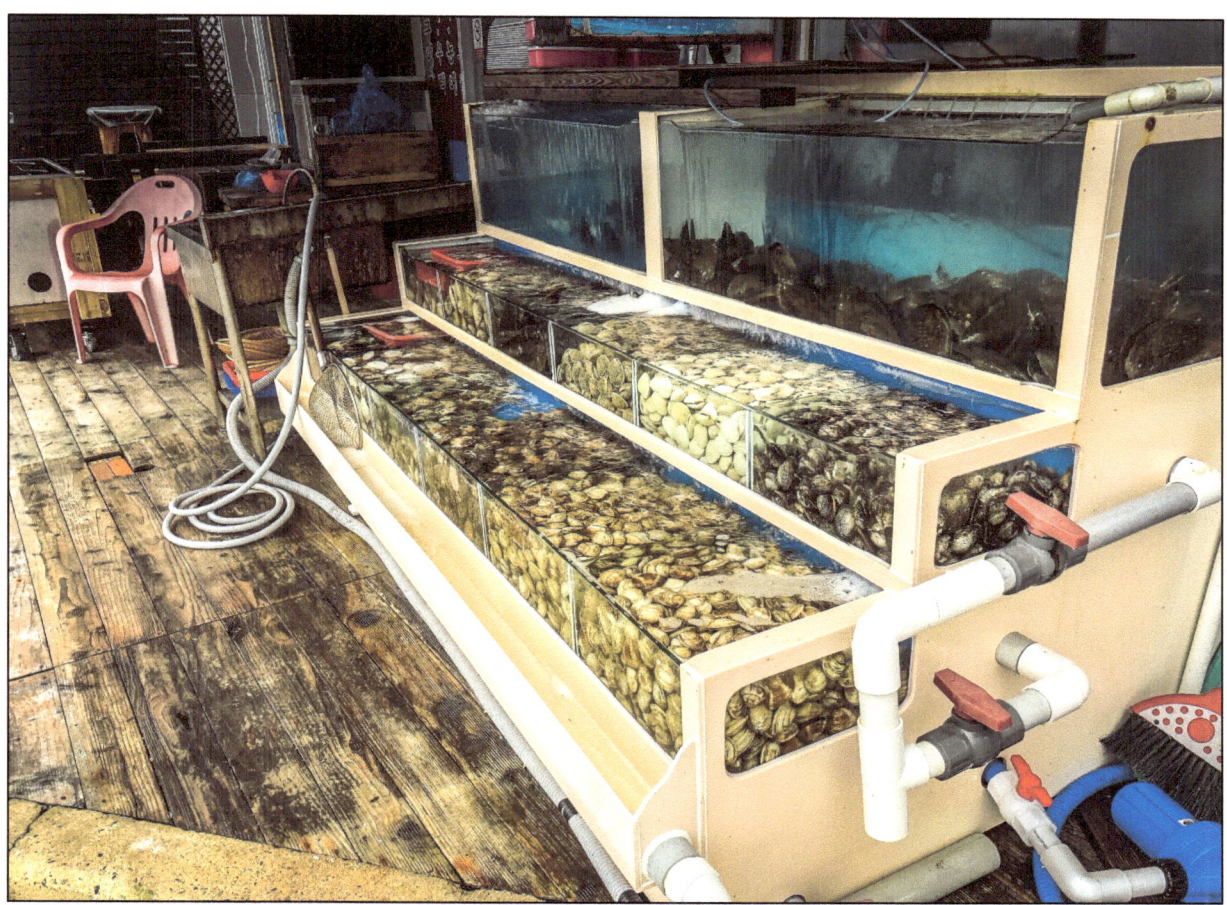

*Farm fresh*
산지 직송의

# Echo Beach

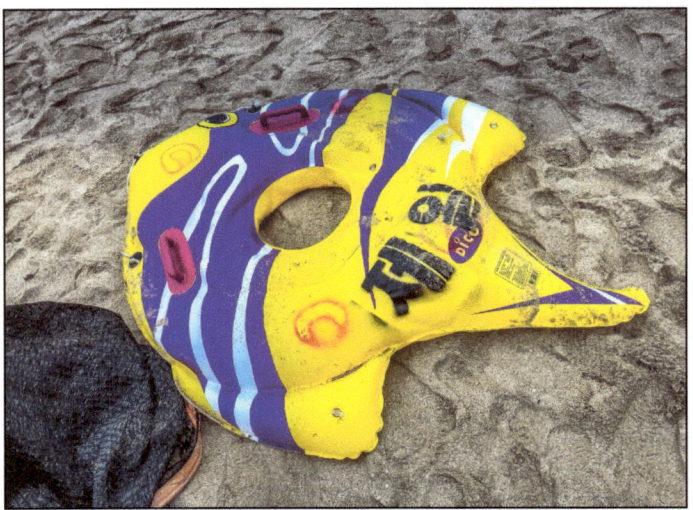

*Brevi herbae aere impleta supernatet*
공기로 채워진 짧은 꼬리 플로트

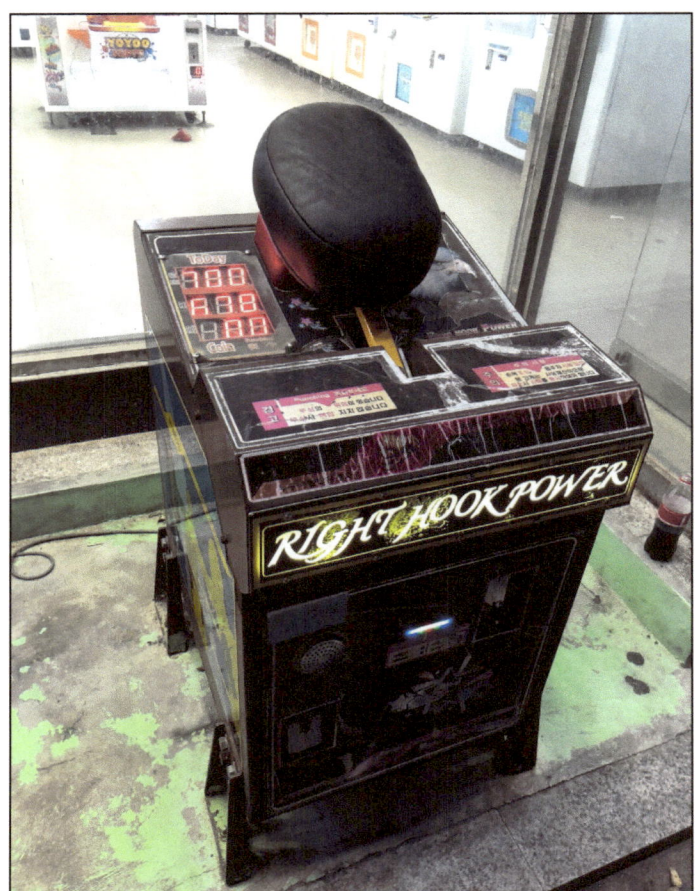

*King hit*
강력한 펀치

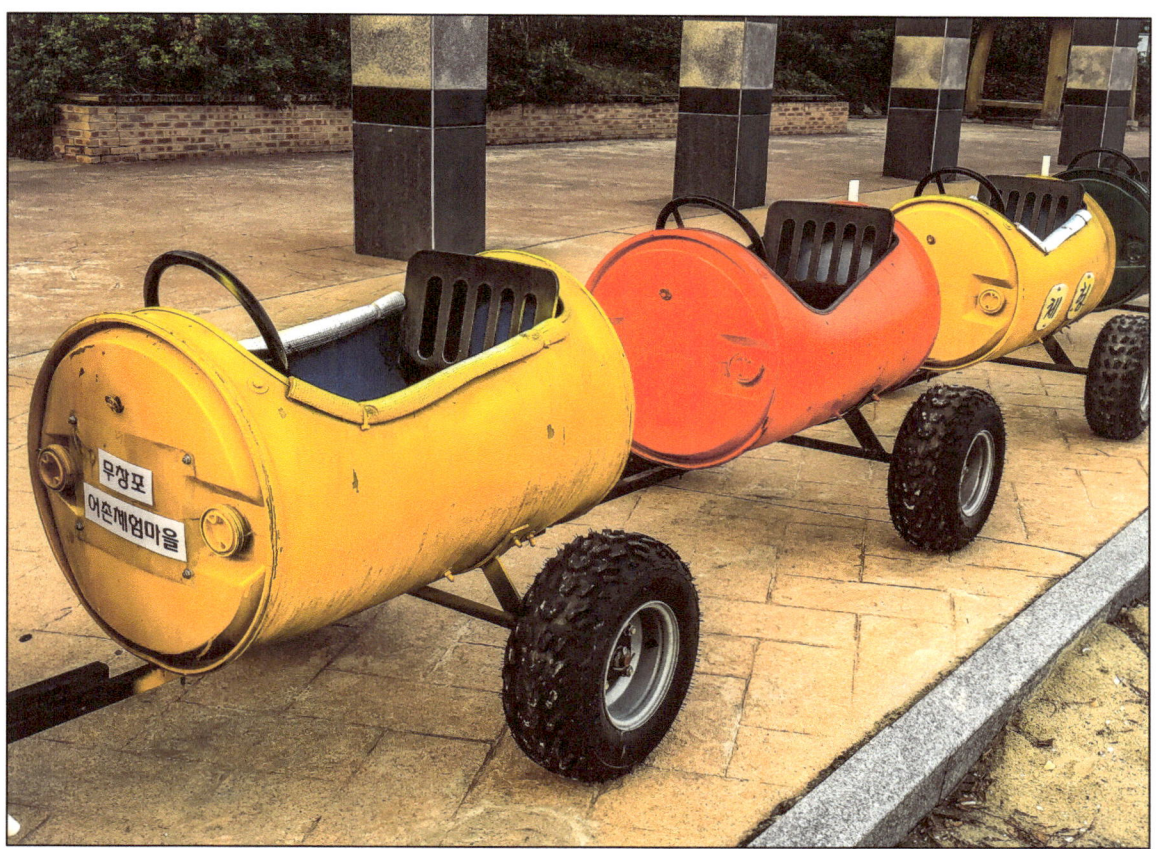

*Barrel ride*
배럴 모양의 놀이기구

Echo Beach

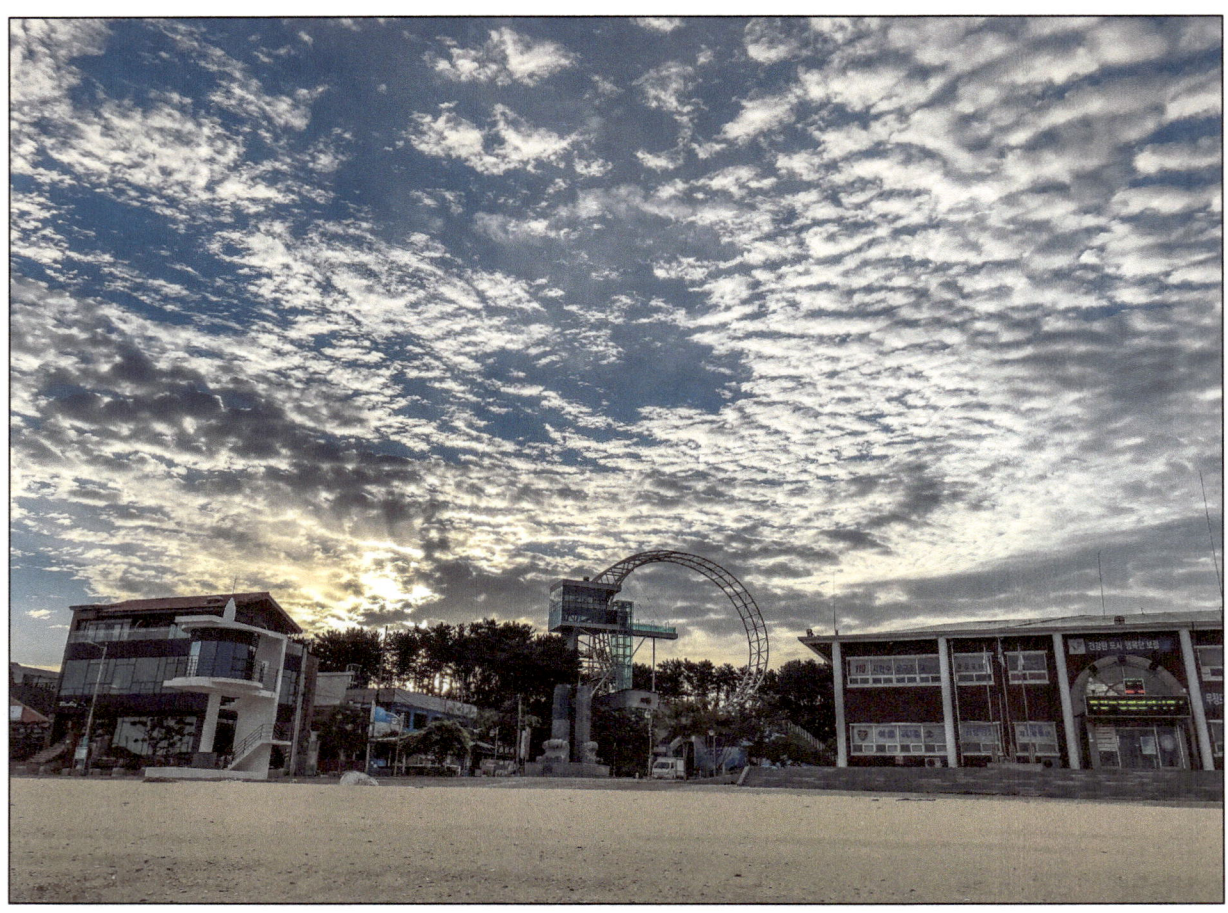

*The beginning*
시작

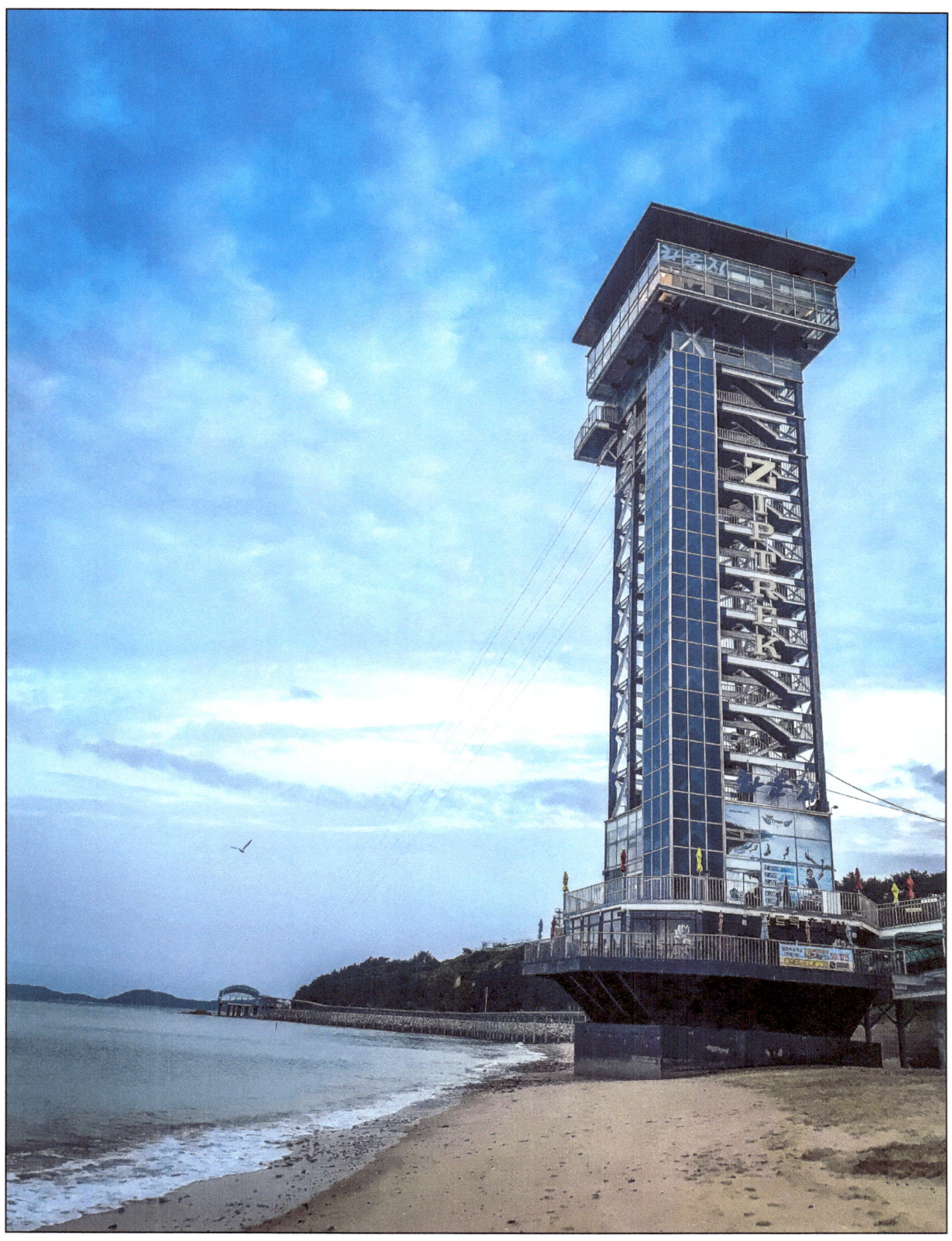

*Tower of travel*
여행의 탑

# Echo Beach

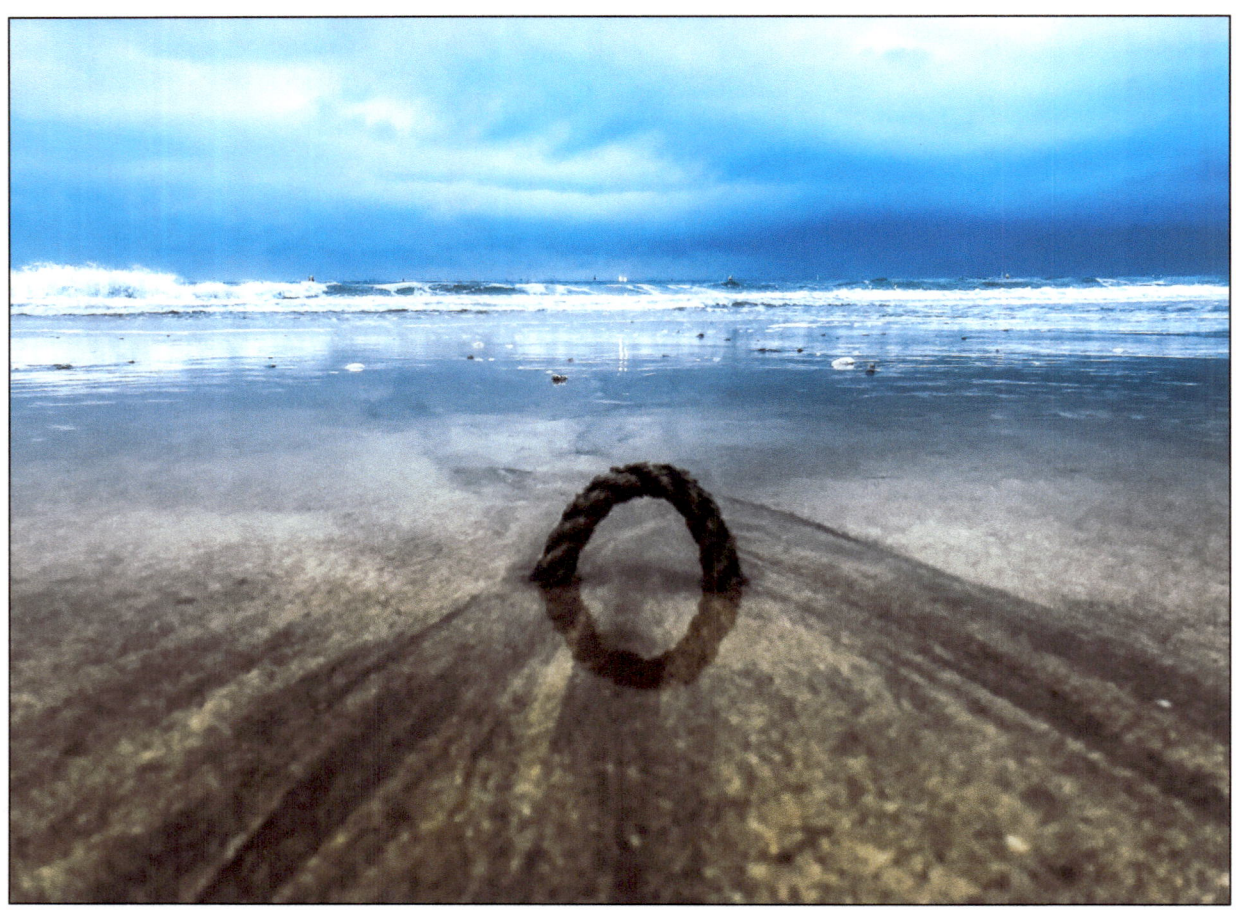

*Caught in the undertow*
저류에 걸린

*Seohae Mon Amour*

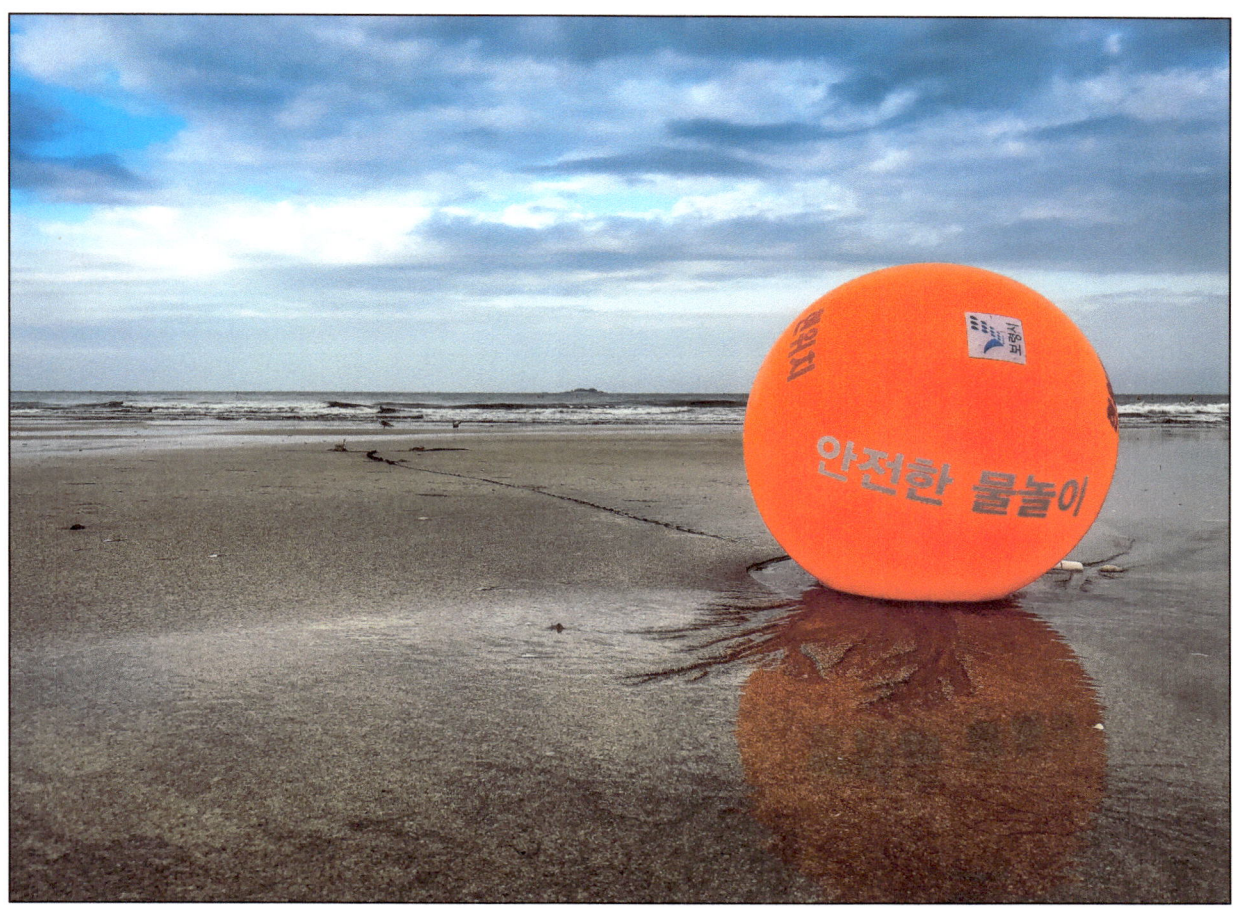

*Safe water*
안전 수역

# Echo Beach

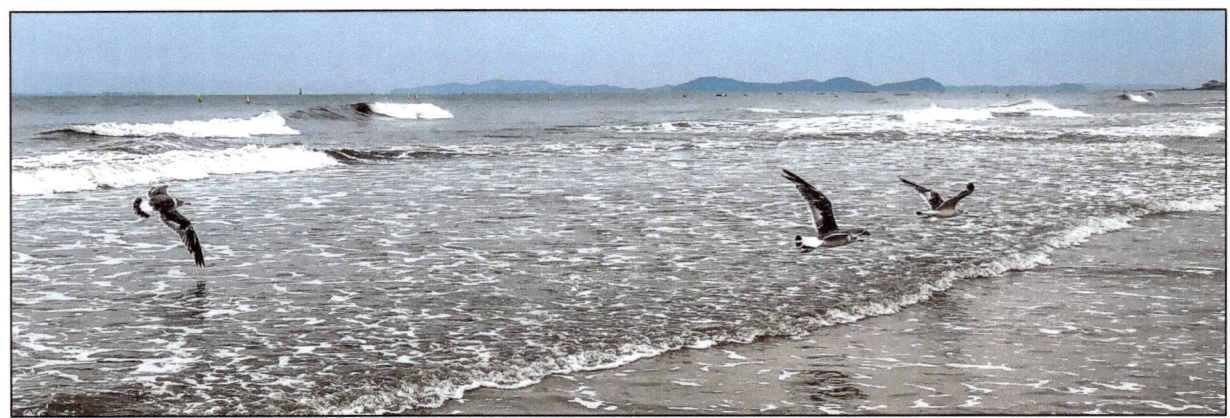

*Overflight*
상공비행

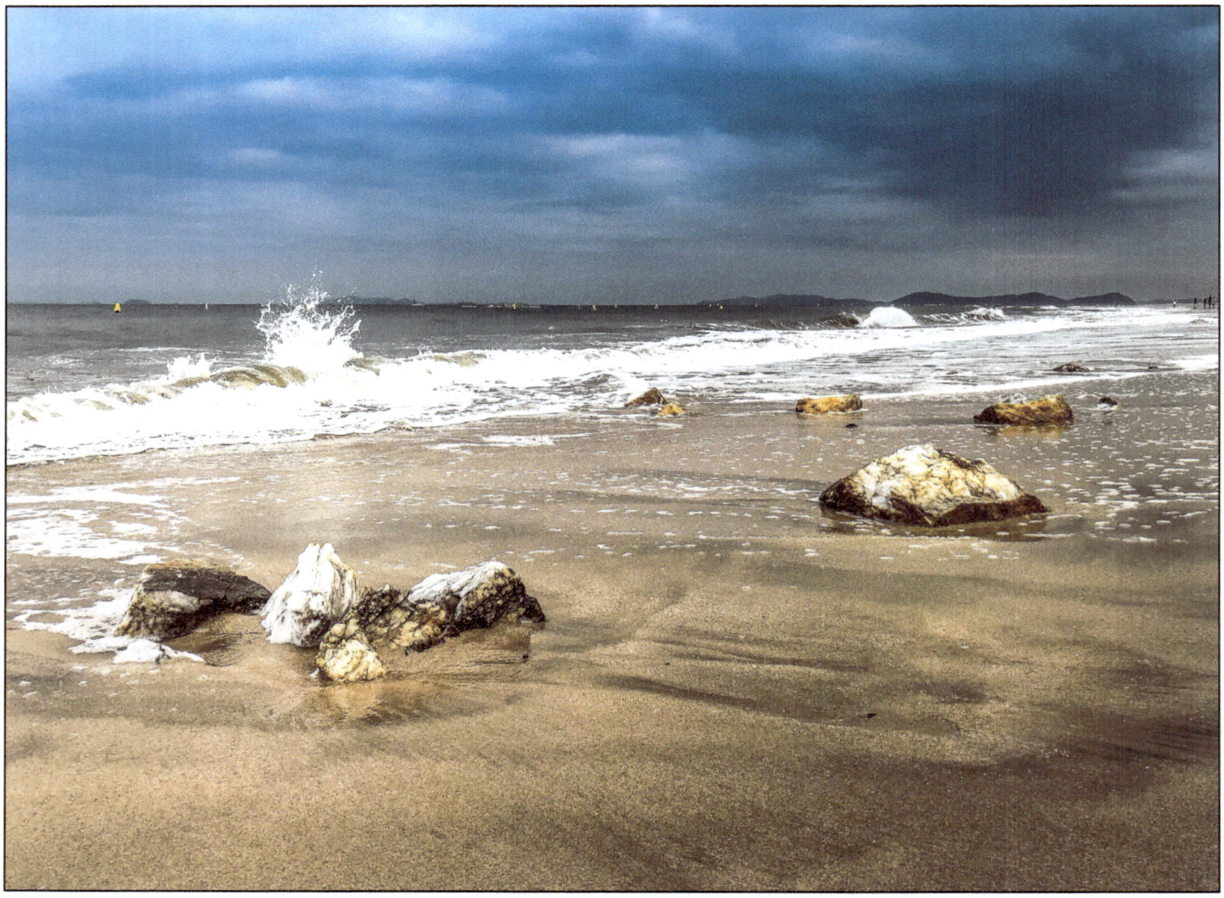

*On the rocks*
바위 위에

*Seohae Mon Amour*

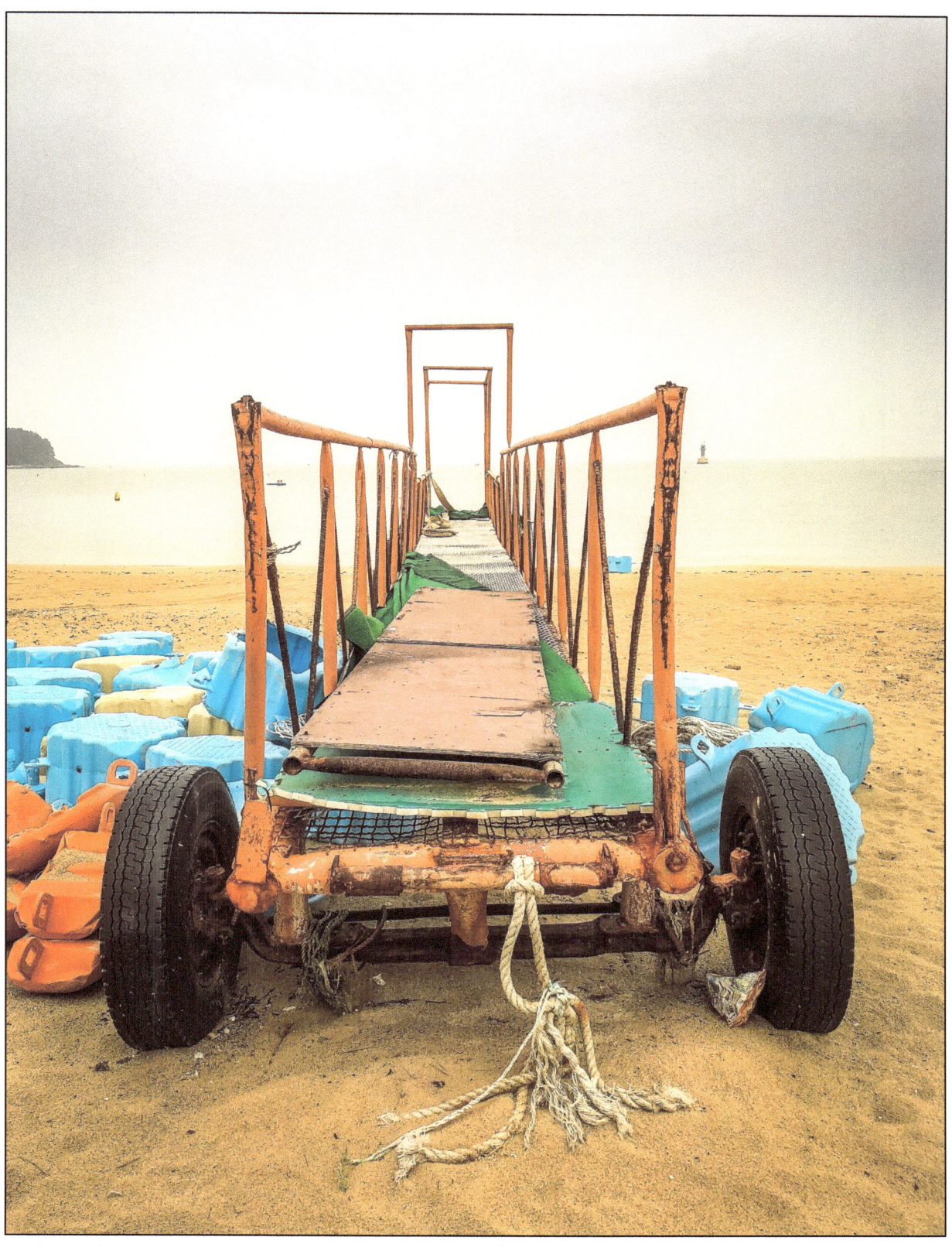

*Road to nowhere*
갈 곳 없는 길

# Ecology

The ecology of the Yellow Sea is collapsing. However, the Yellow Sea Marine Ecosystem Project, an initiative led by the United Nations Development Program, is designed to assist the regions three stakeholders – China, North Korea and South Korea – in realizing environmentally-sustainable use and management of the sea and its watershed. The aim is to reduce developmental stress and promote sustainable exploitation of the ecosystem from a heavily urbanized, industrialized, and densely populated shelf sea.

# 생태계

황해의 생태계가 붕괴되고 있습니다. 그러나, 유엔개발계획(UNDP)에 의해 진행된 황해 해양 생태계 프로젝트는 중국, 북한, 한국 3 곳의 지역 이해 당사자들이 바다와 그 바다 유역의 환경친화적 지속가능한 이용과 관리를 실현하도록 지원합니다. 목표는 개발상의 스트레스를 줄이고 심하게 도시화되고 산업화된, 인구 밀도가 높은 대륙붕 바다에서 생태계의 지속적인 개발을 촉진하는 것입니다.

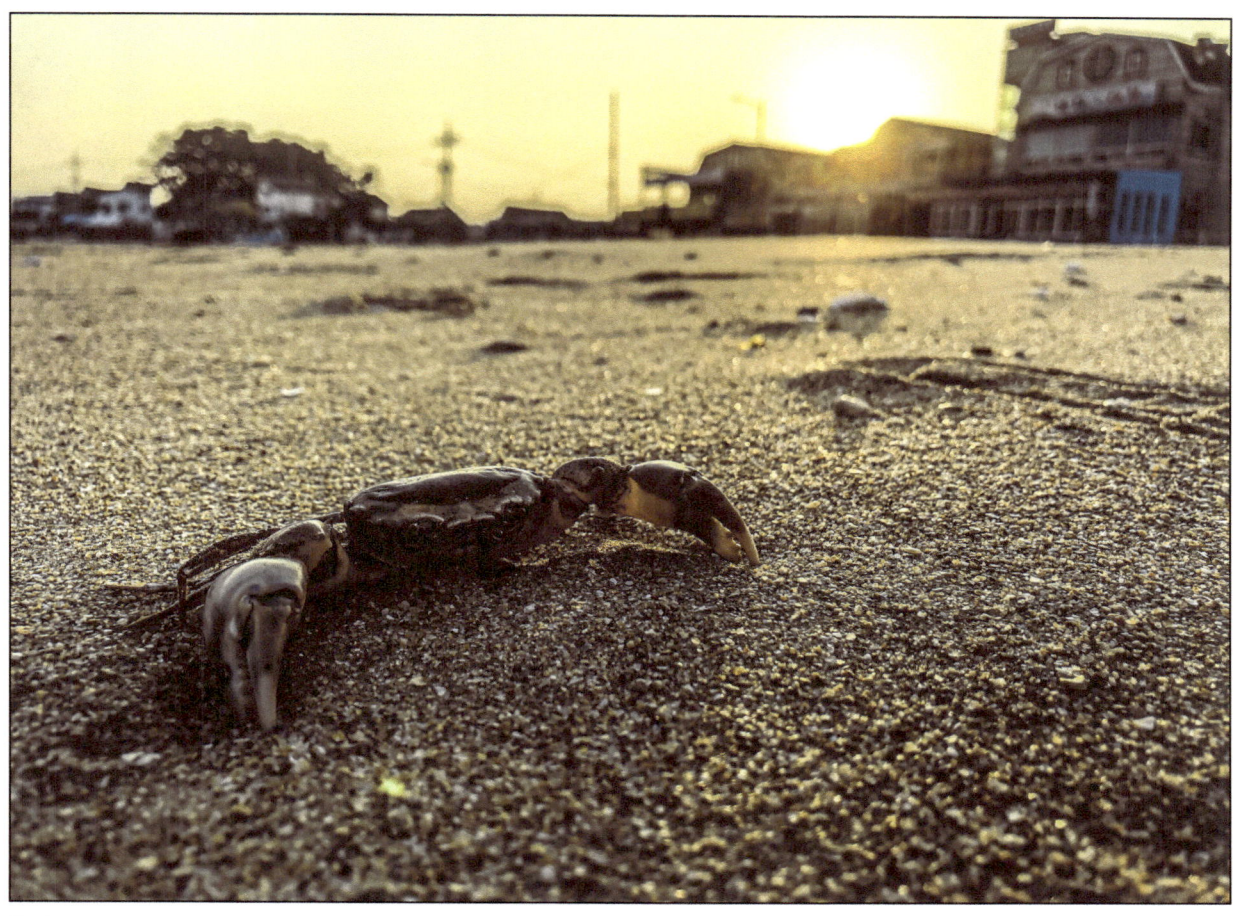

*Crab*
게

# Echo Beach

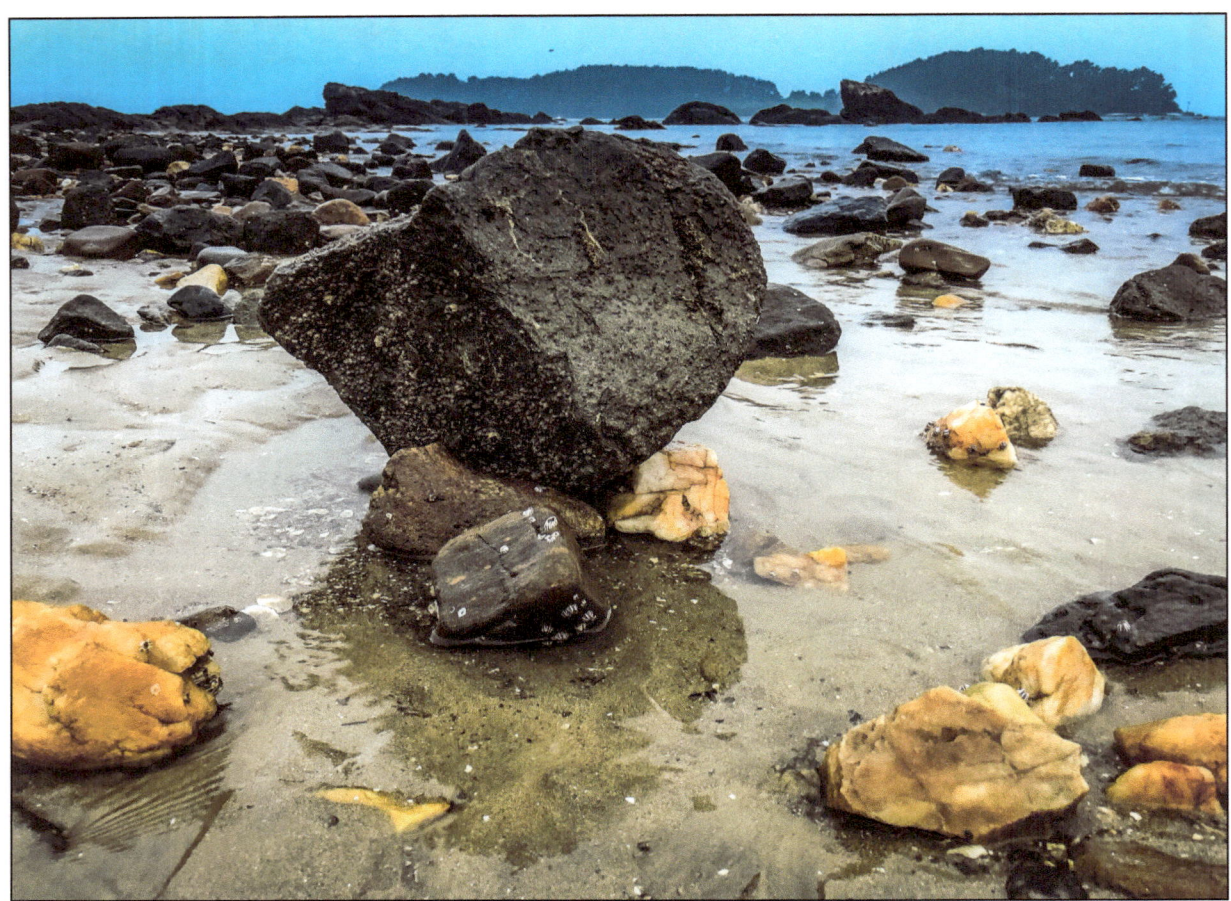

*Dolmon*
돌몬

*Seohae Mon Amour*

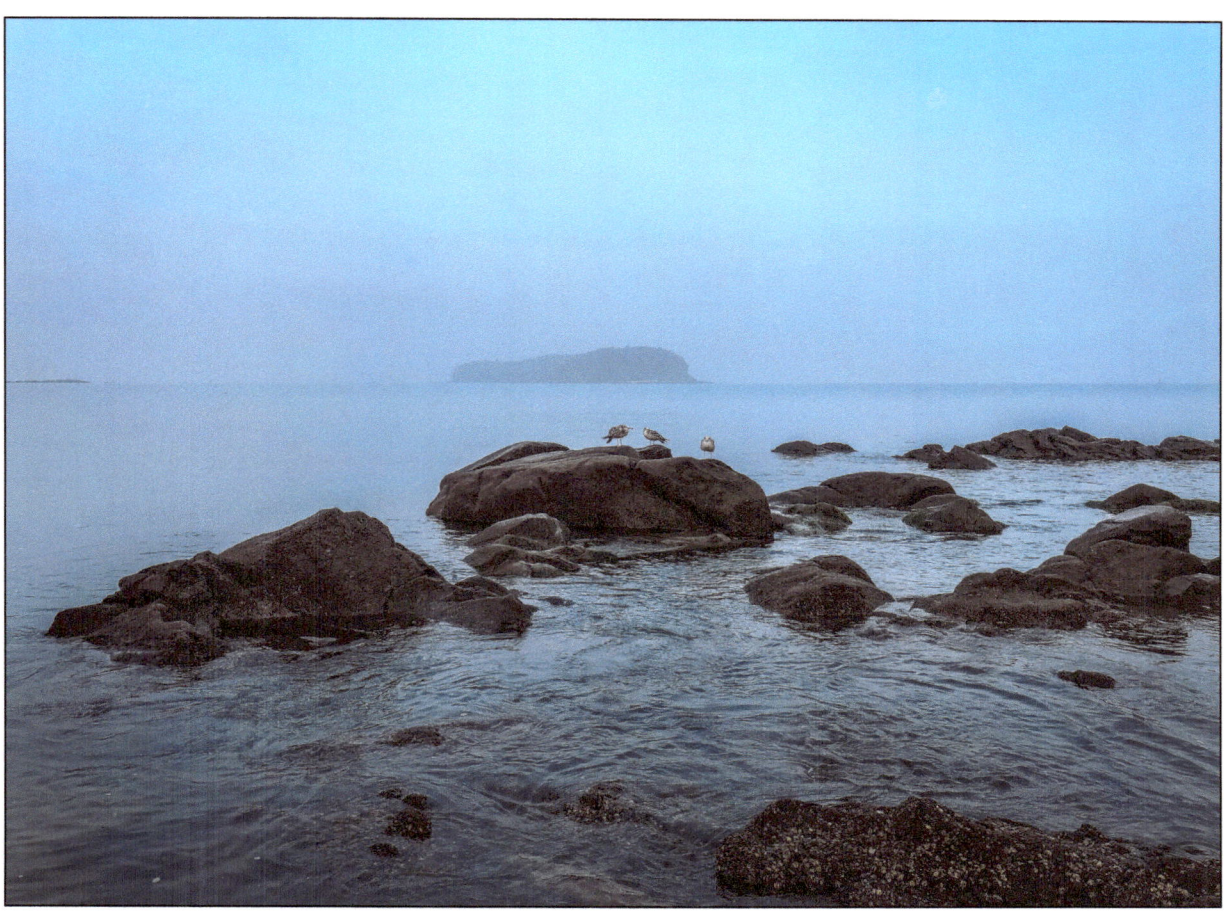

*The birds*
새들

# Echo Beach

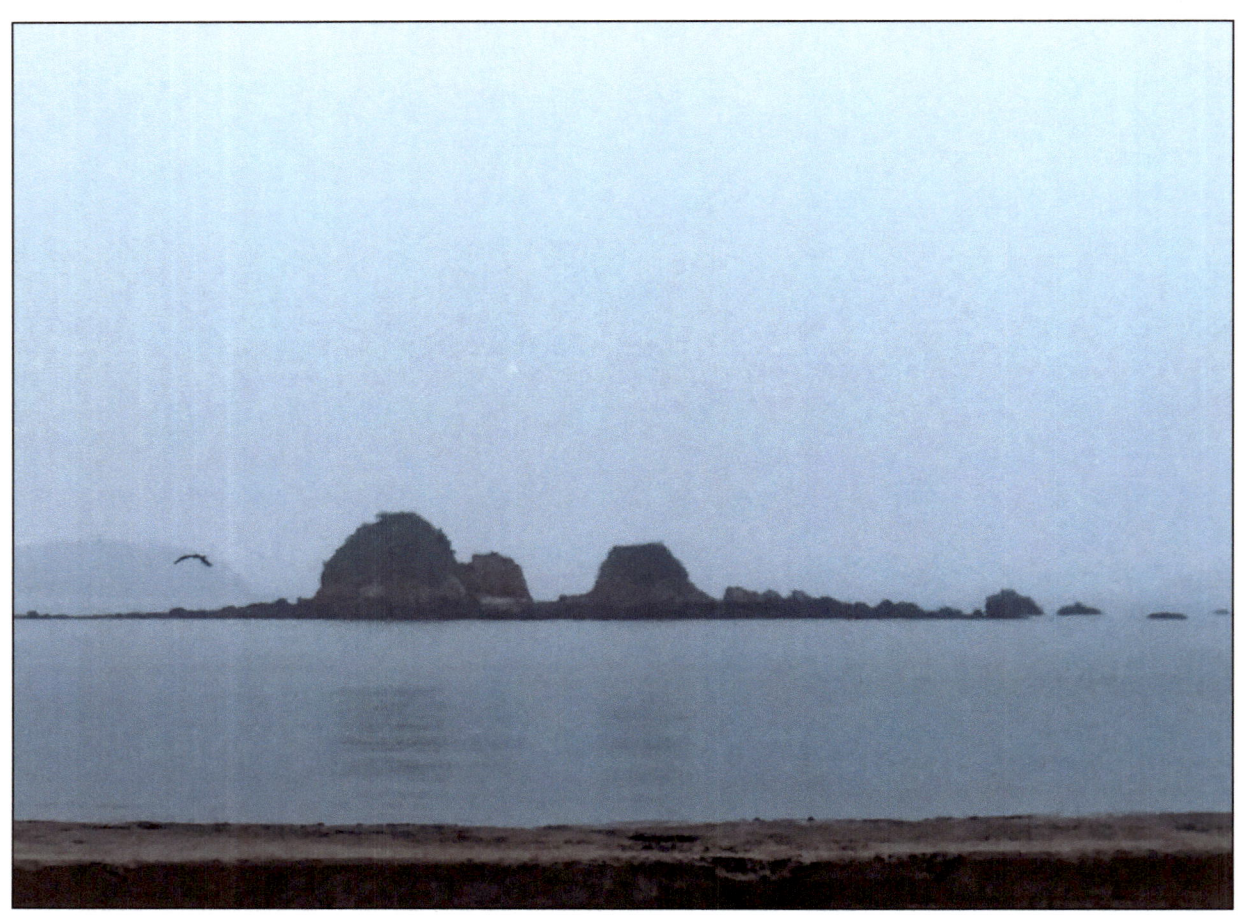

*Fantasy island*
환상의 섬

*Seohae Mon Amour*

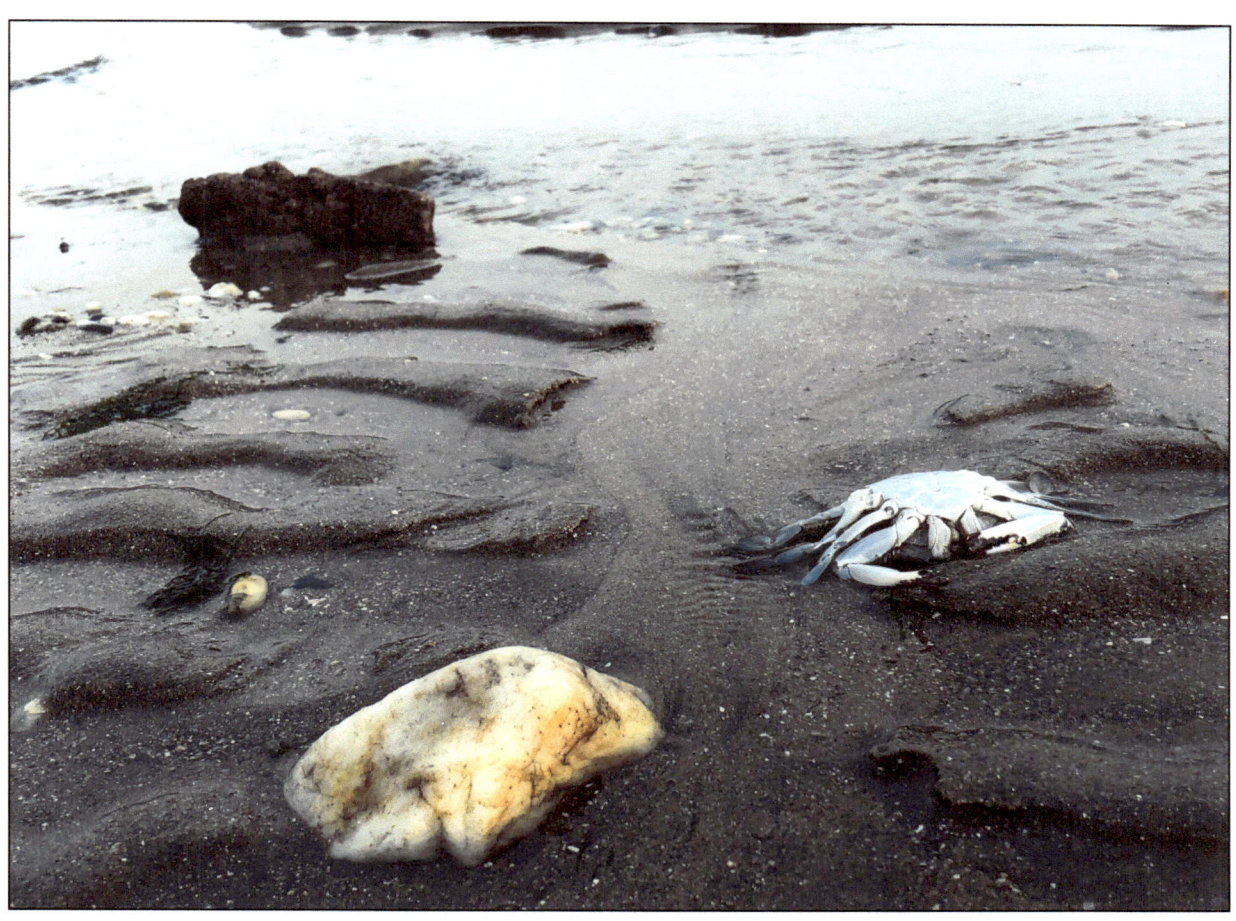

*Keeled over*
뒤집힌

# Echo Beach

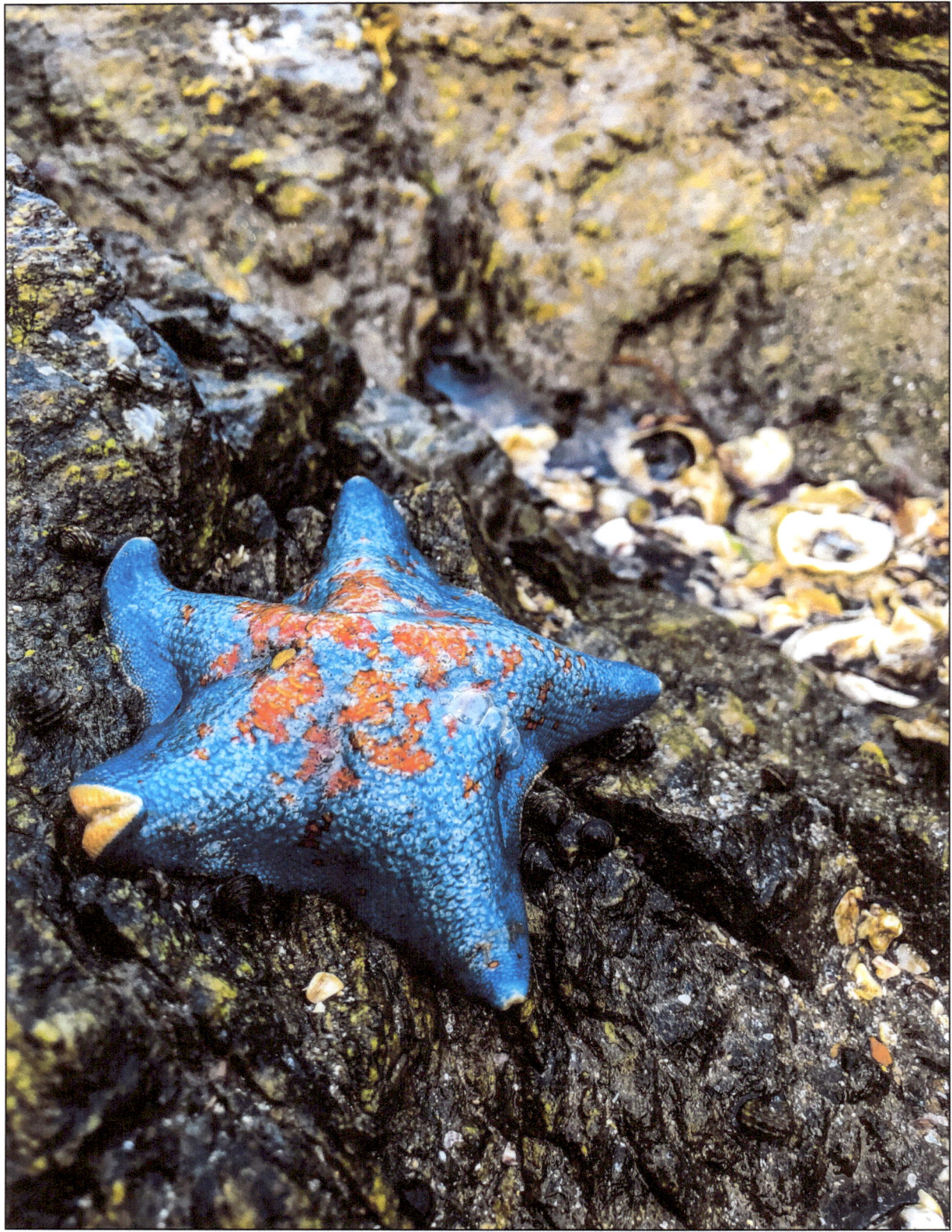

*LB – Lucky Bluestar*
LB – 럭키 블루스타

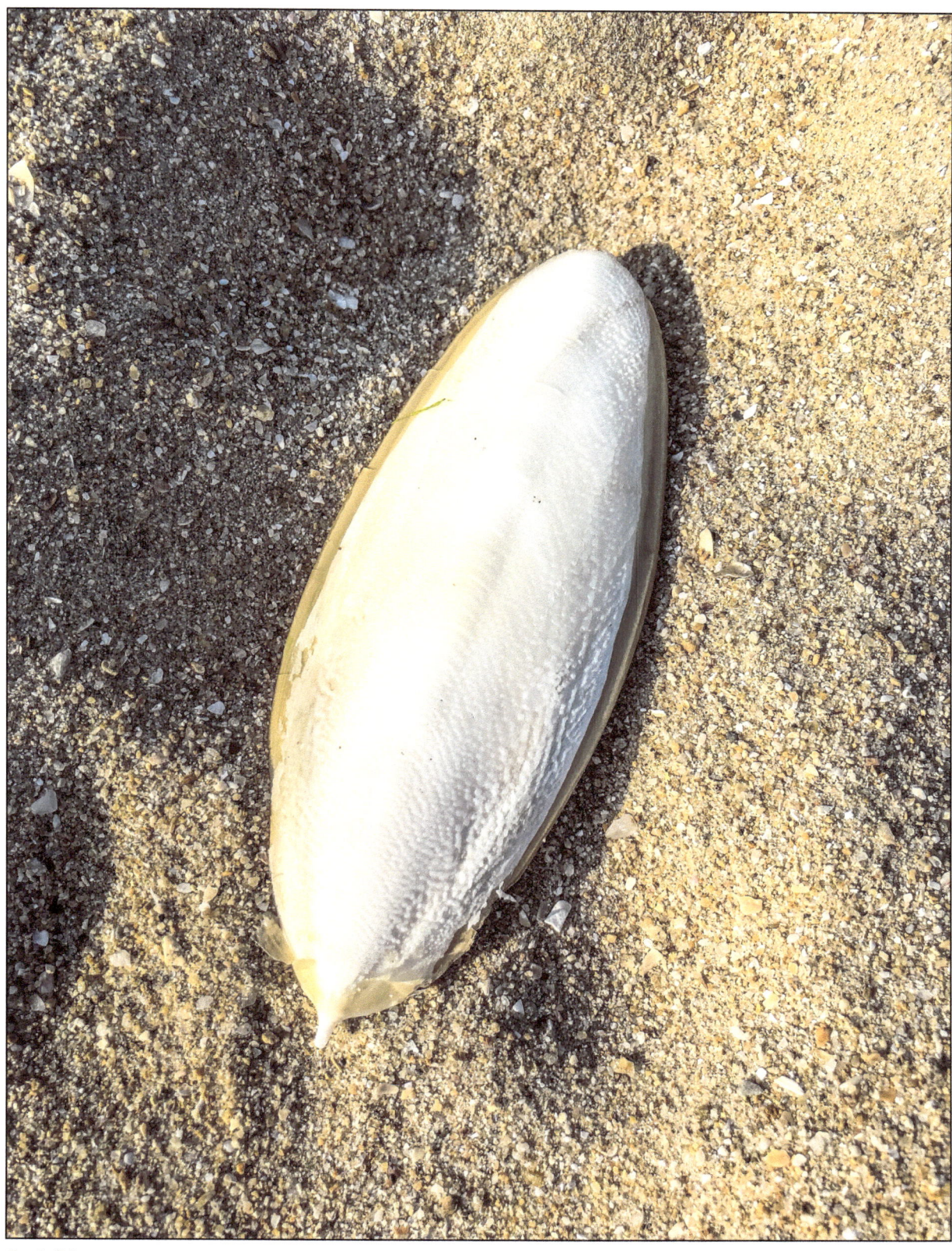

*Cuttlefish*
갑오징어

# Echo Beach

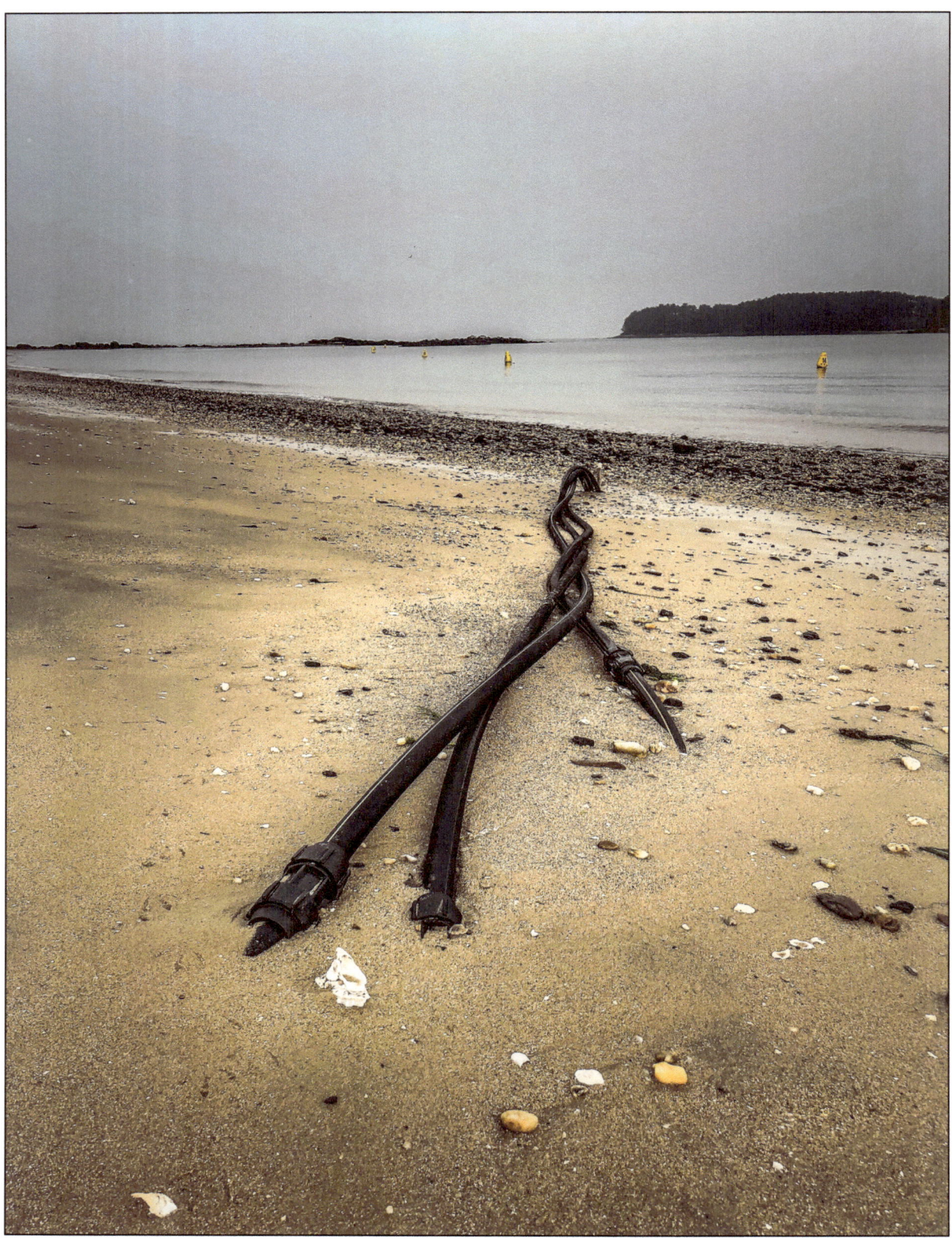

*Lifelines*
생명선

*Seohae Mon Amour*

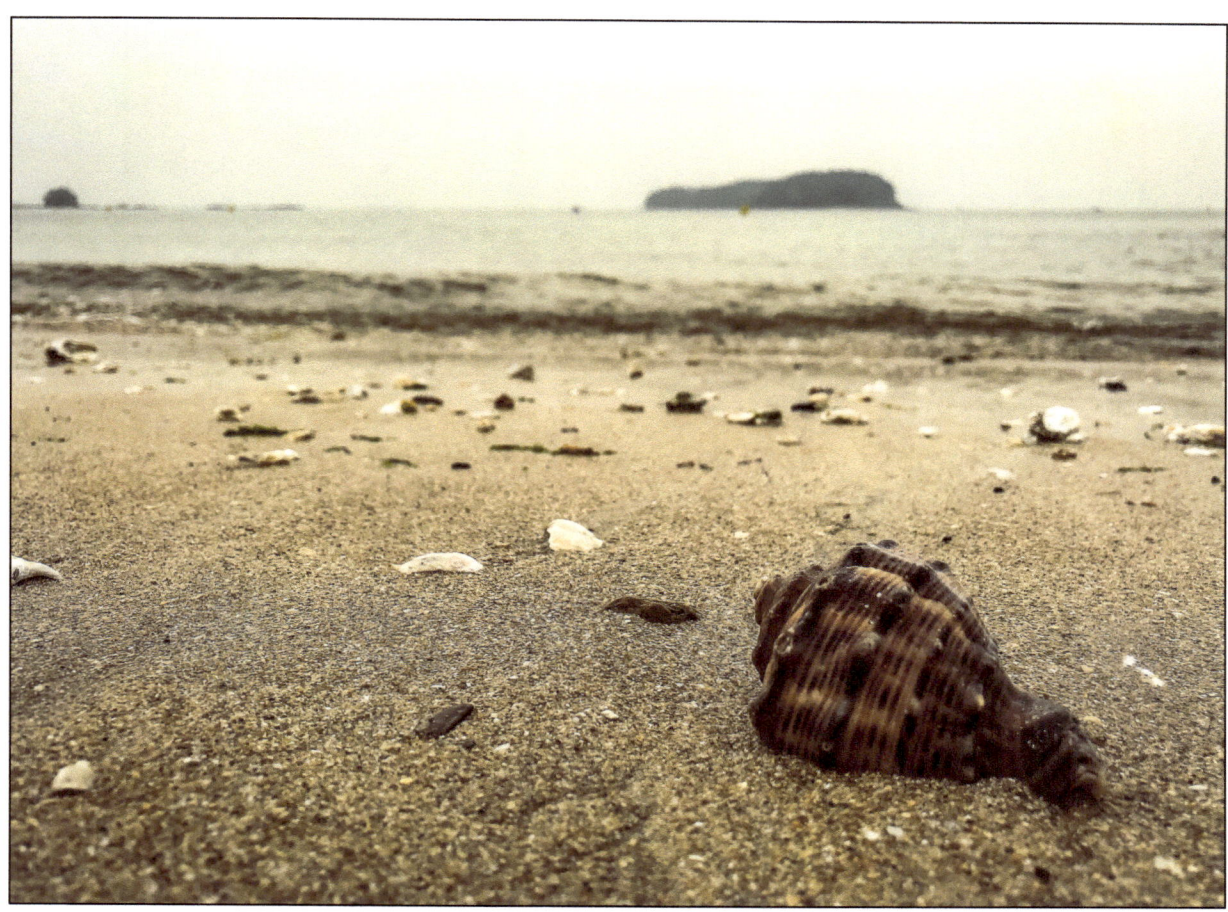

*Shell shock*
셸 쇼크

73

# Echo Beach

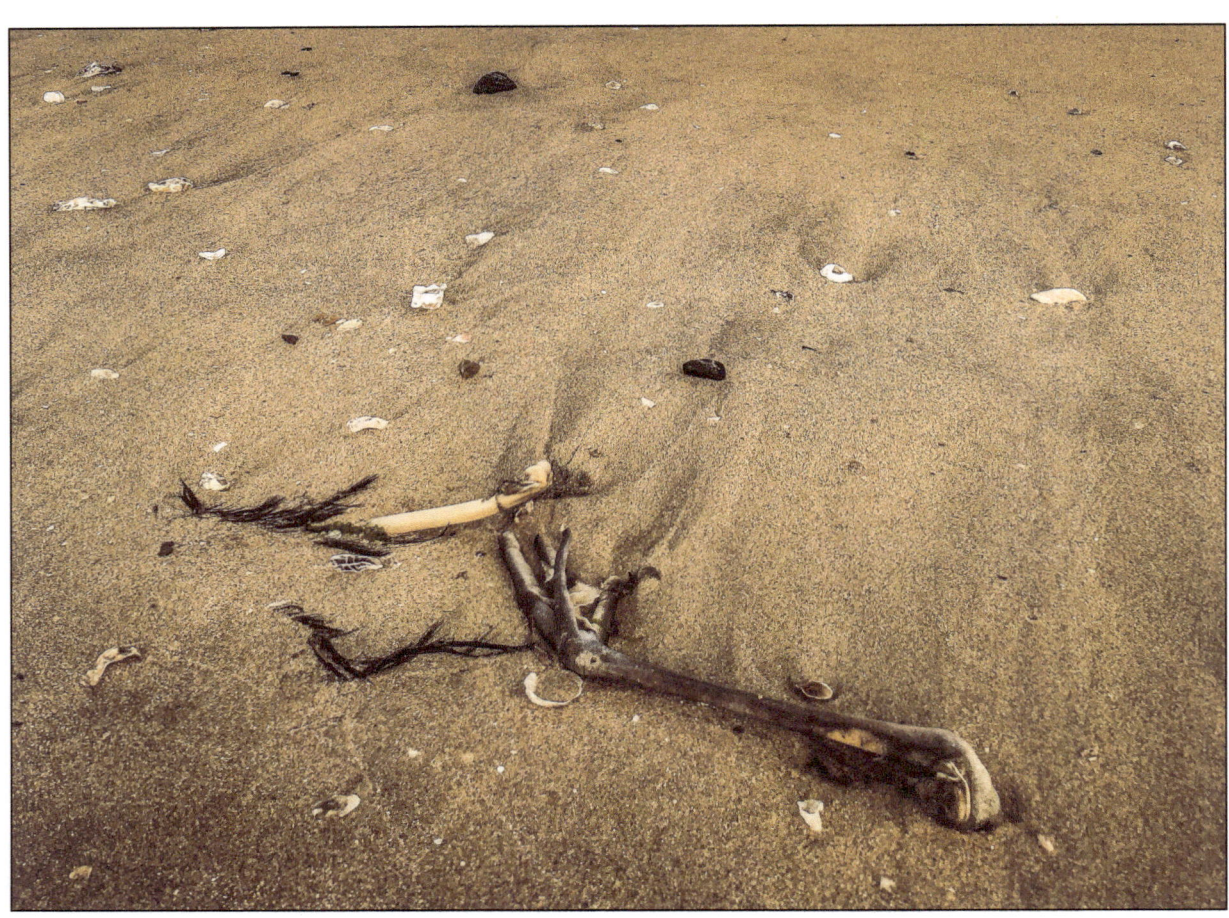

*Cold feet*
차가운 발

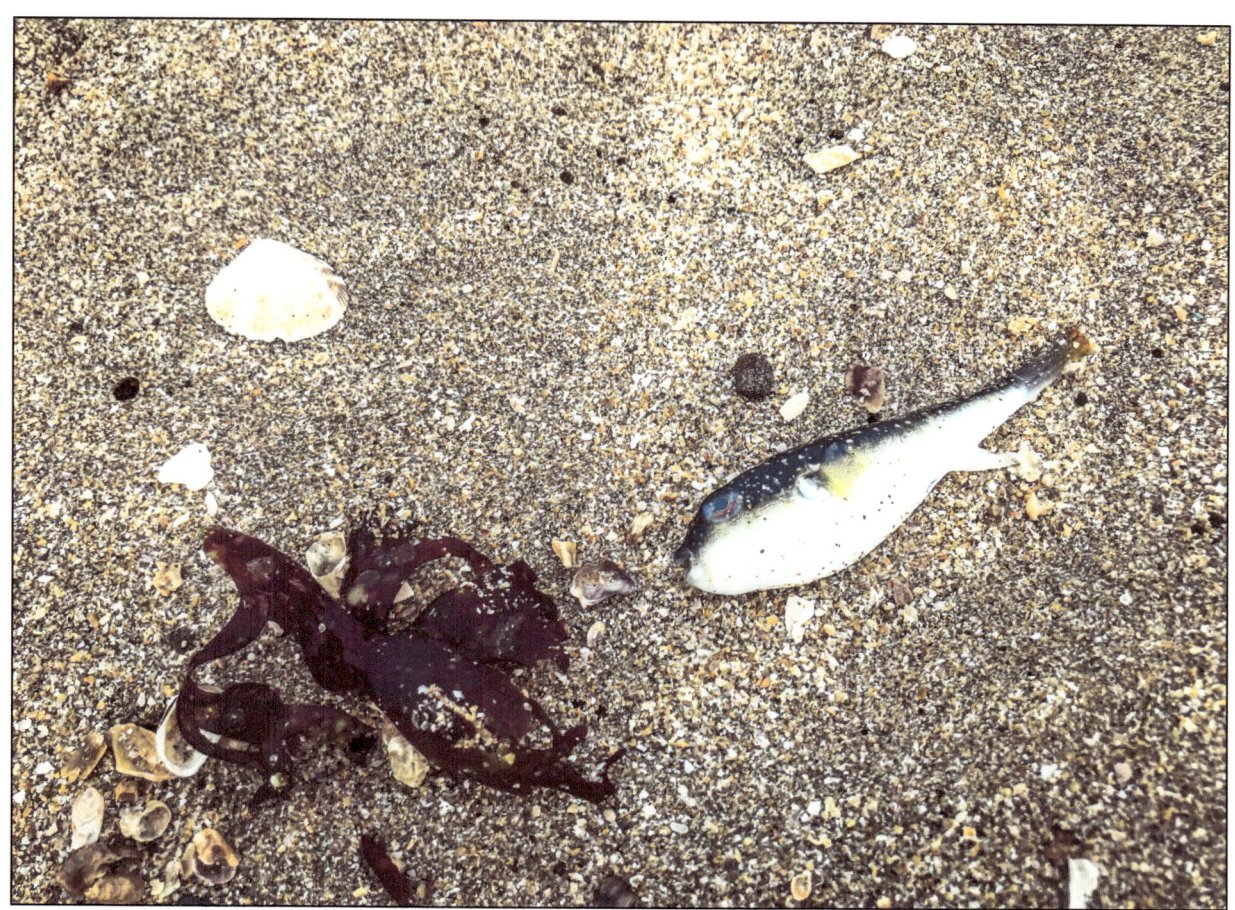

*Tetraodontidae with kelp and shells on sand*
조개껍데기와 해초와 있는 모래 위 복어

Echo Beach

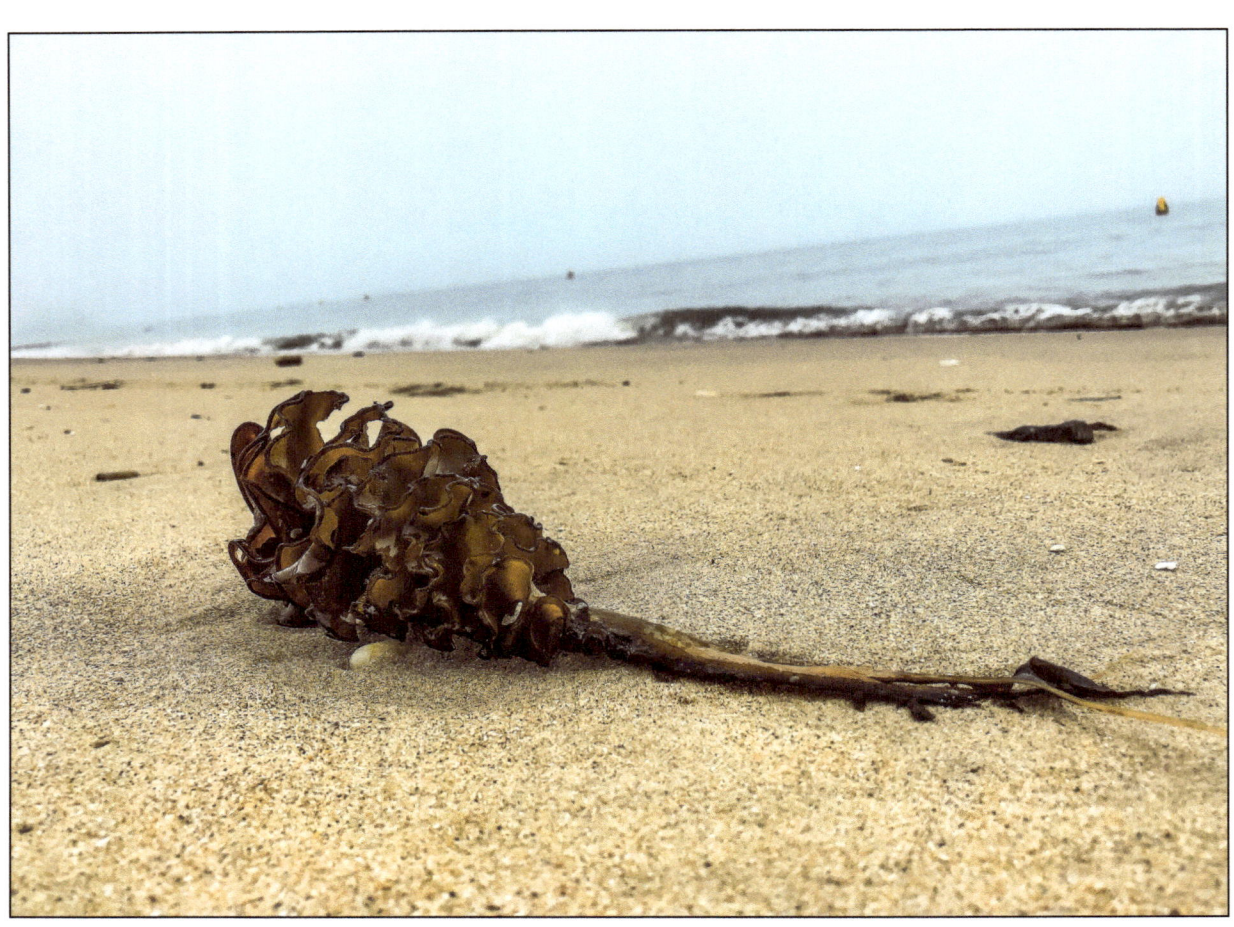

*Flagellation*
채찍질

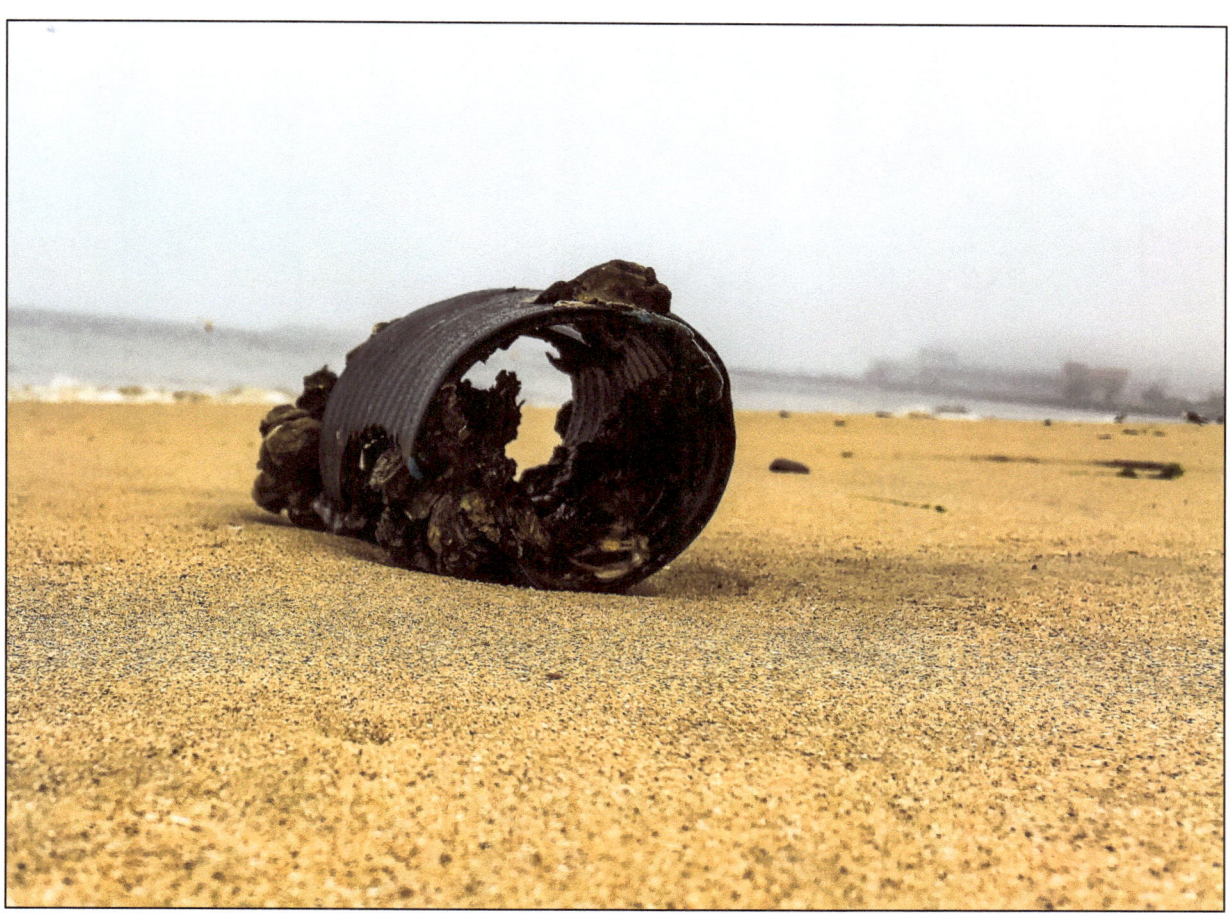

*Tunnel vision*
터널시

Echo Beach

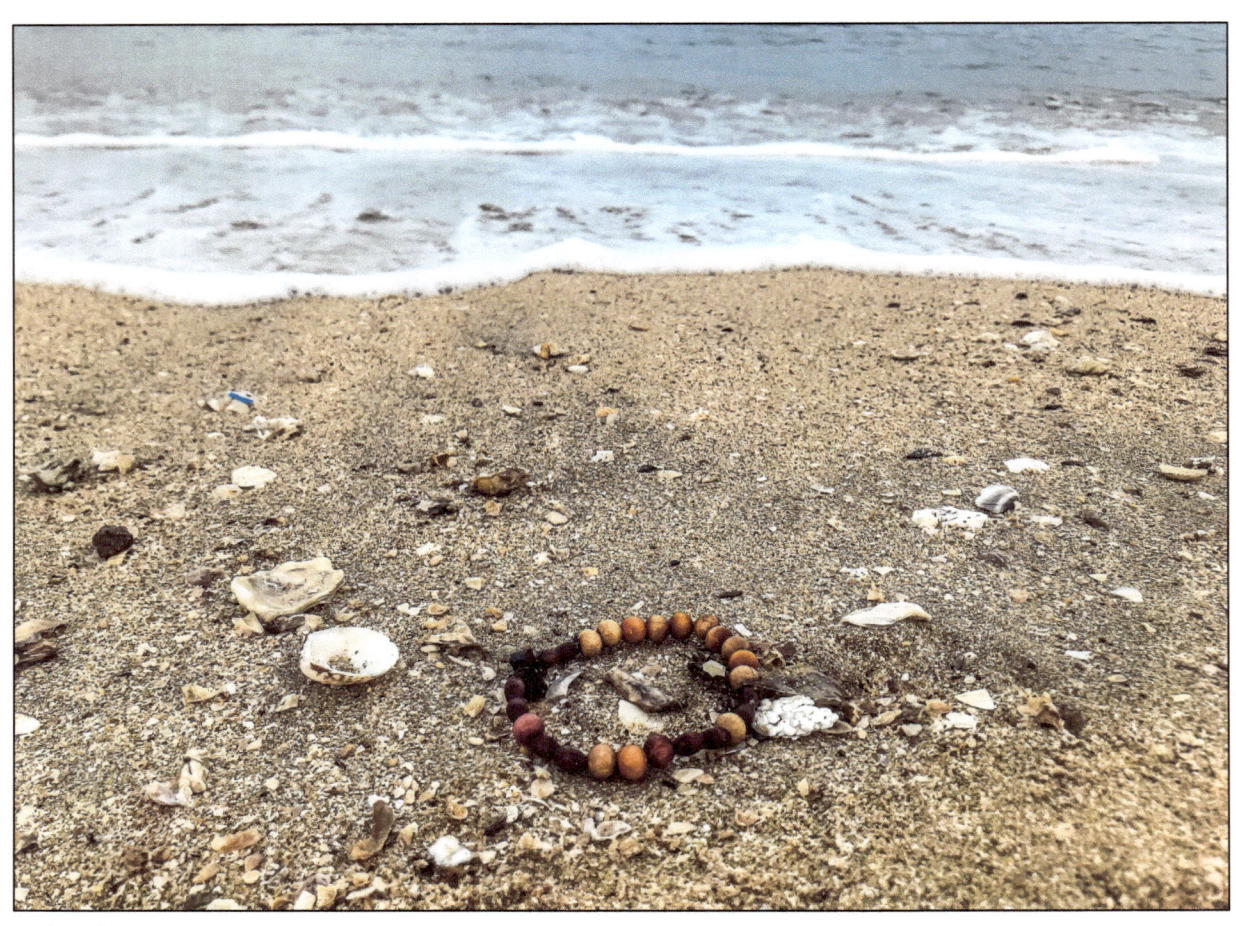

... *full of grace*
은총이 가득찬…

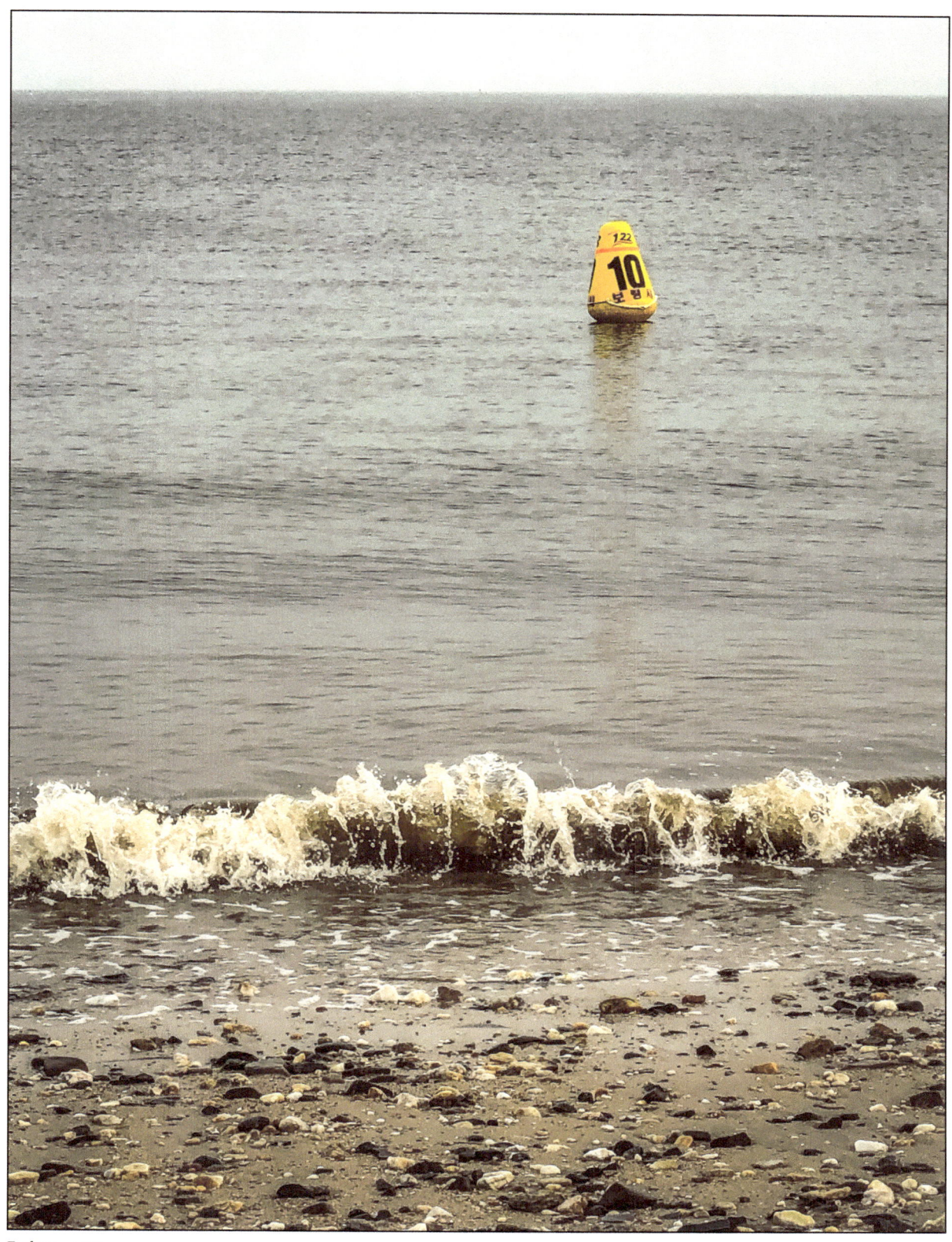

*Refuse no.10*
10 번을 거절하다

# Refuse

The original idea behind the collection of these images was to document the refuse found along the shores of the western coast that is uniquely Korean. However, as the previous images illustrate, there was so much more that made these Korean shores unique. The reality remains, pollution along the coastline of the Western Sea is widespread. Some debris washes ashore, but much is taken and left behind, discarded. It is hoped that the following imagery will help to inspire those who go to these shores to take out what they take in, and to perhaps also take away much more than memories of their visit when they leave.

# 폐물

이 사진들을 모은 원래 생각은 독특하게 위치한 서쪽 연안의 해안을 따라 발견된 쓰레기를 문서화하는 것이었습니다. 그러나, 이전의 사진이 보여주고 있듯이 훨씬 더 많은 것들이 이 해안을 독특하게 만들어 주고 있었습니다. 서해의 해안지대를 따라 오염은 널리 퍼져있다는 사실이 남았습니다. 일부 쓰레기 잔해가 해안으로 밀려옵니다. 하지만, 옮겨졌거나 두고 왔거나 버려진 것들이 많이 있습니다. 다음의 사진들이 이 해안을 찾는 사람들에게 떠날 때는 자신이 가져온 것은 챙겨 갈 수 있도록 또한 방문 당시의 기억보다 더 많은 것들을 치울 수 있게 자극이 되었기를 바랍니다.

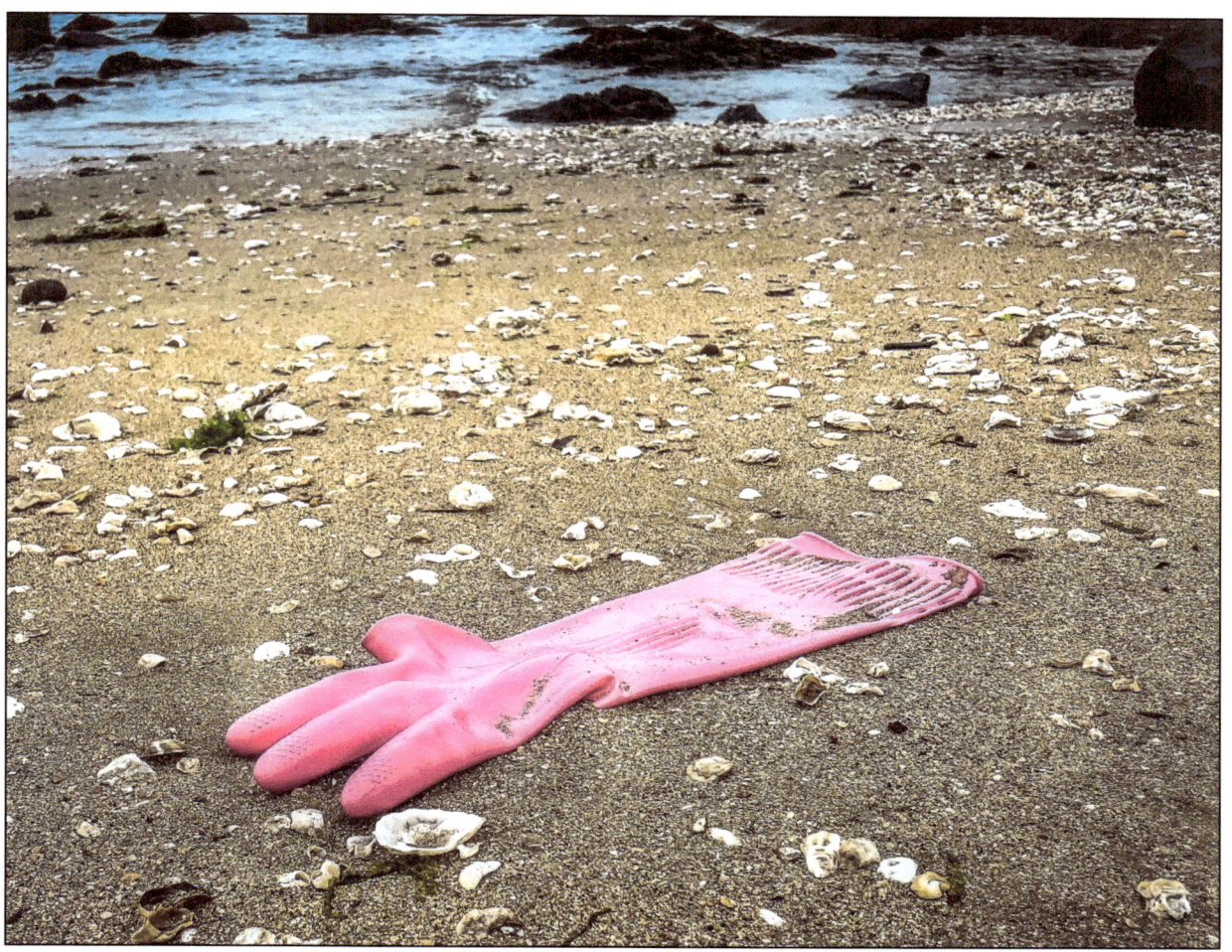

*Mommy's hand*
마미손

Echo Beach

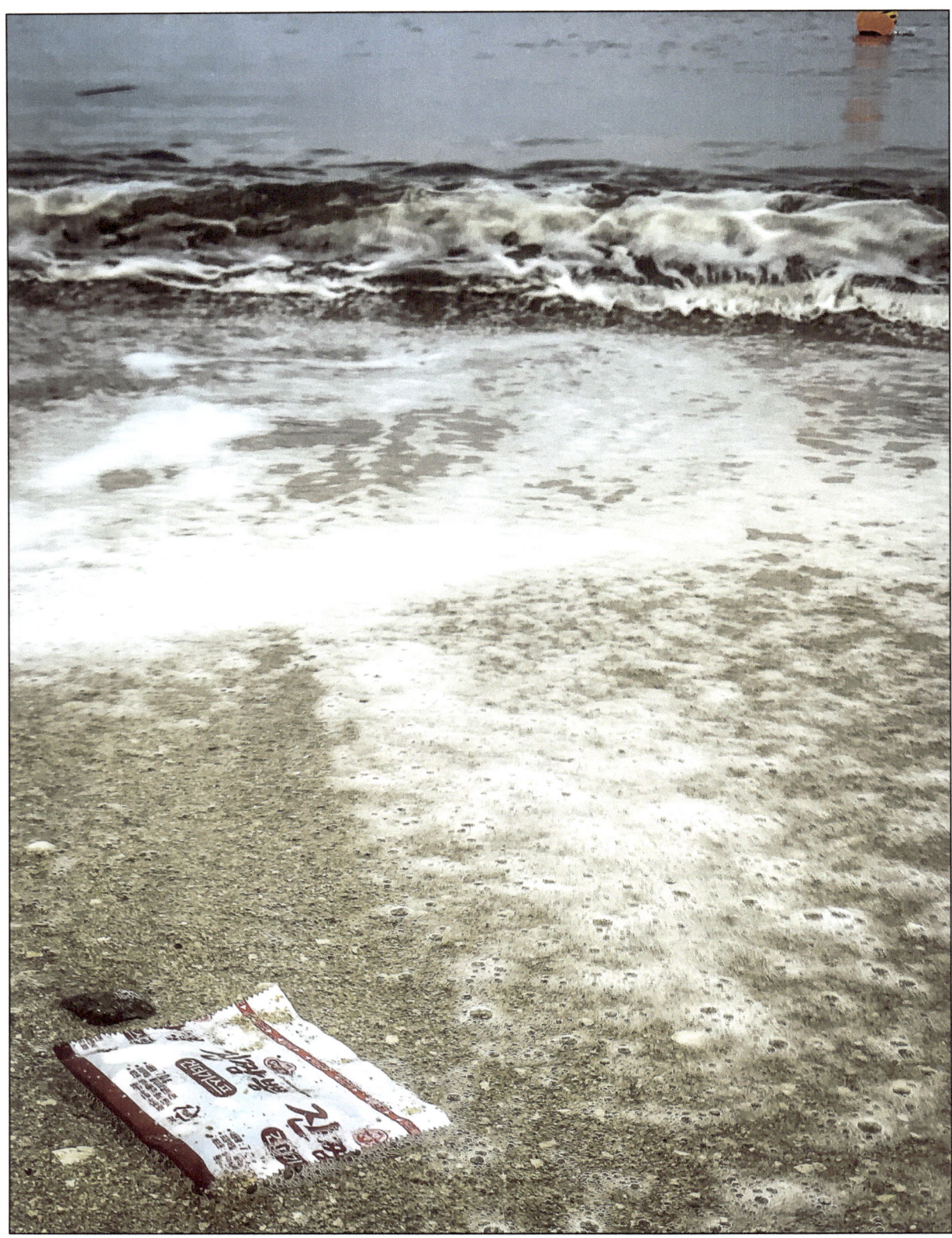

*Ramyeon*
라면

## Seohae Mon Amour

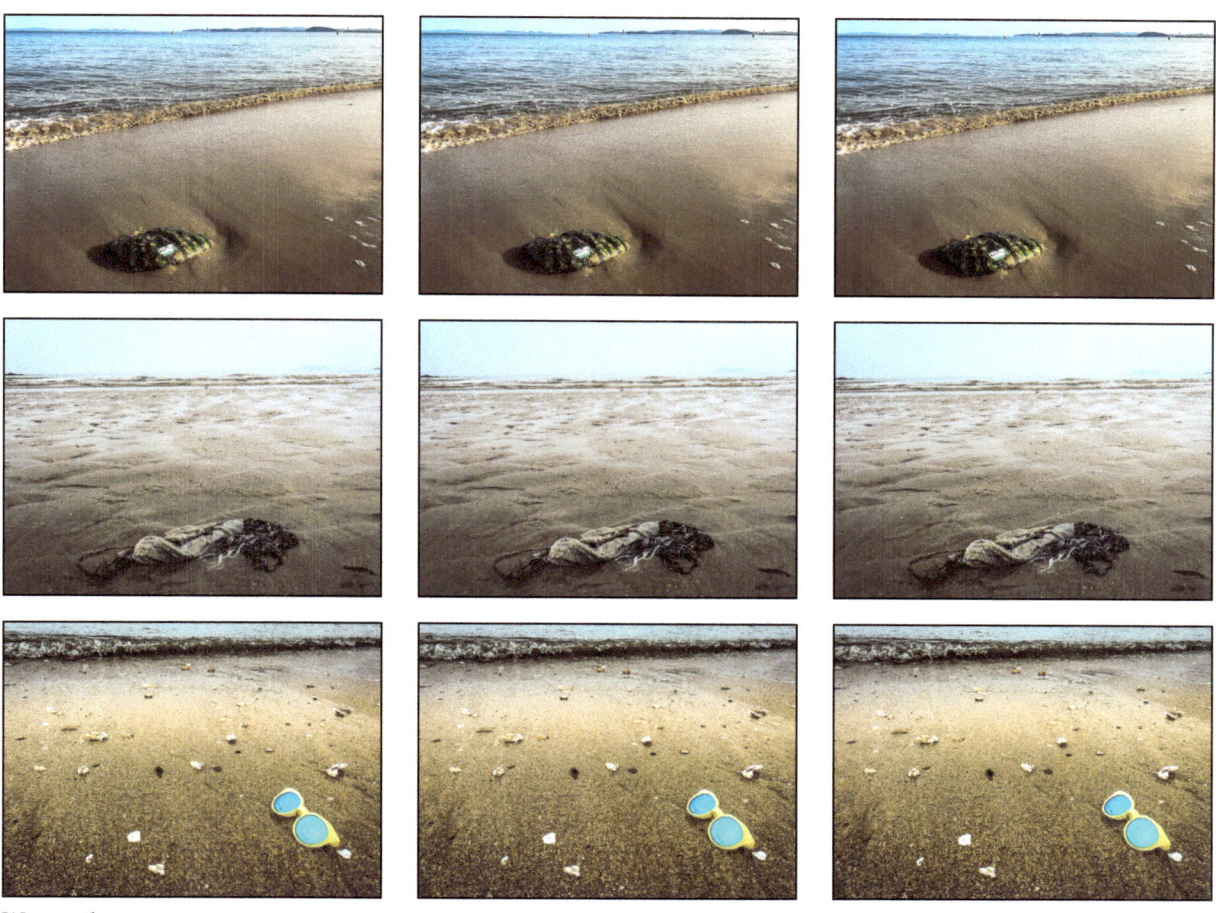

*Watermelon sugar*
수박 설탕

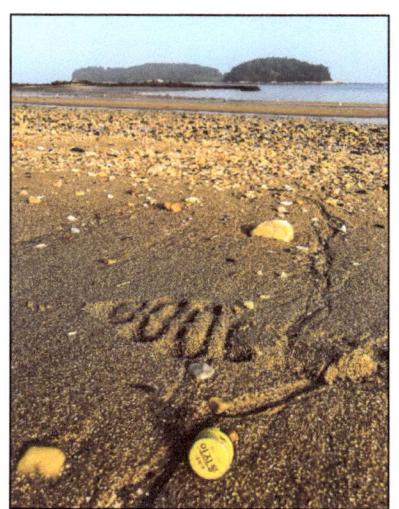

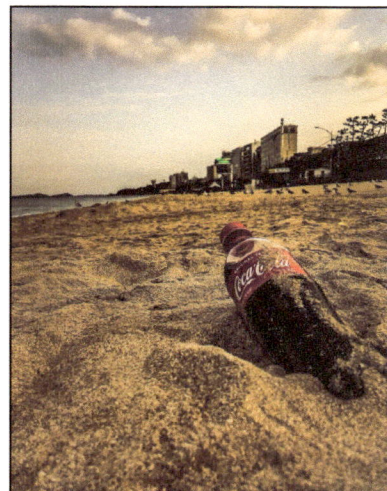

*Elixirs of life*
생명의 묘약

# Echo Beach

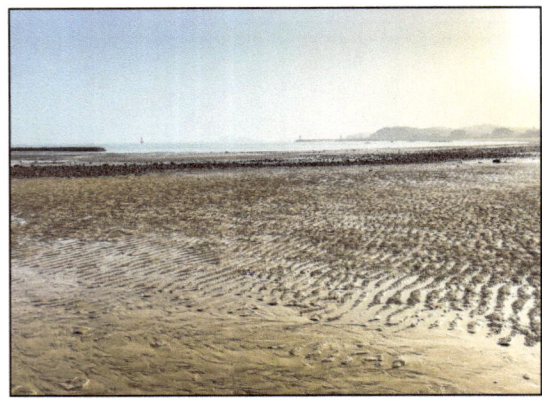

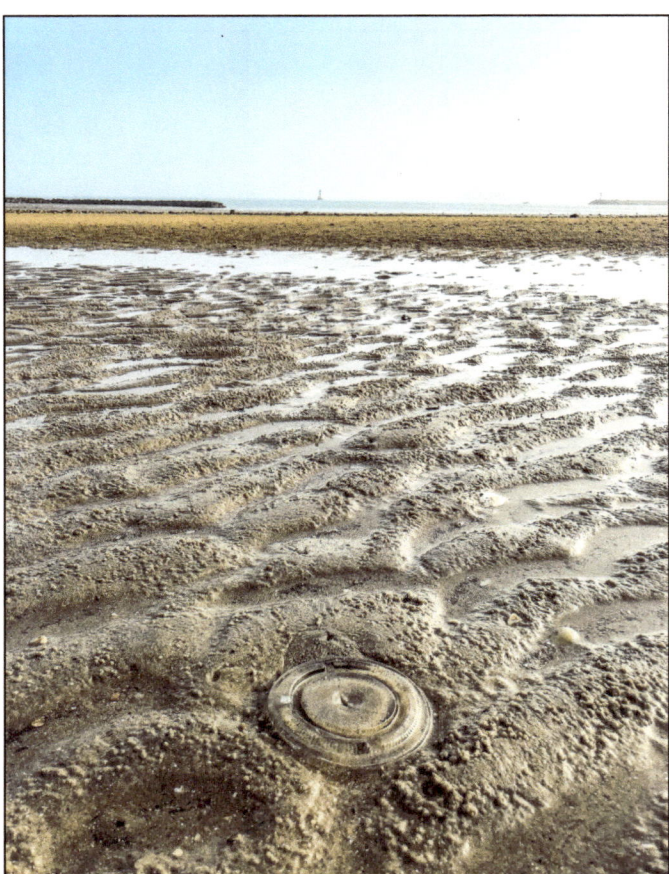

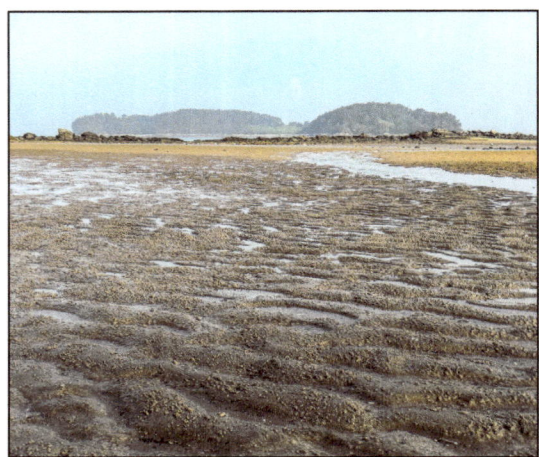

*Thirst*
갈증

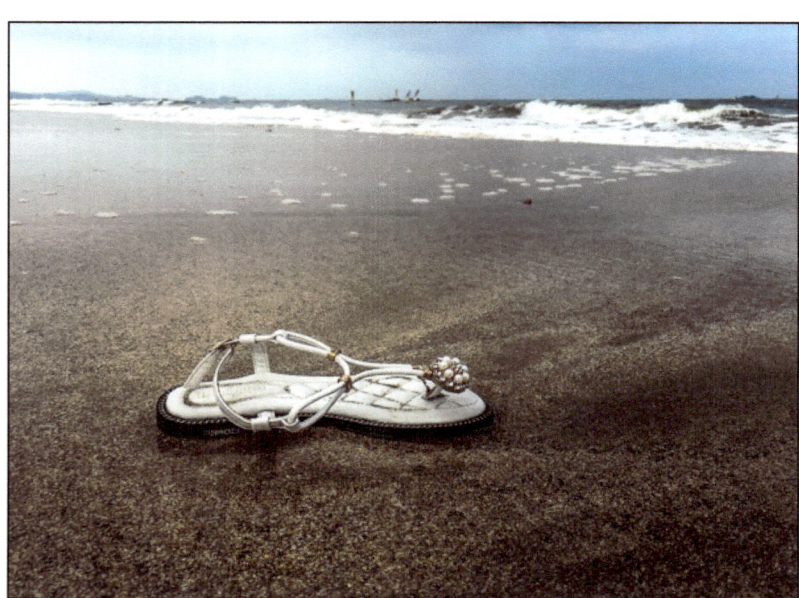

*YehShen's Slipper*
예셴의 신

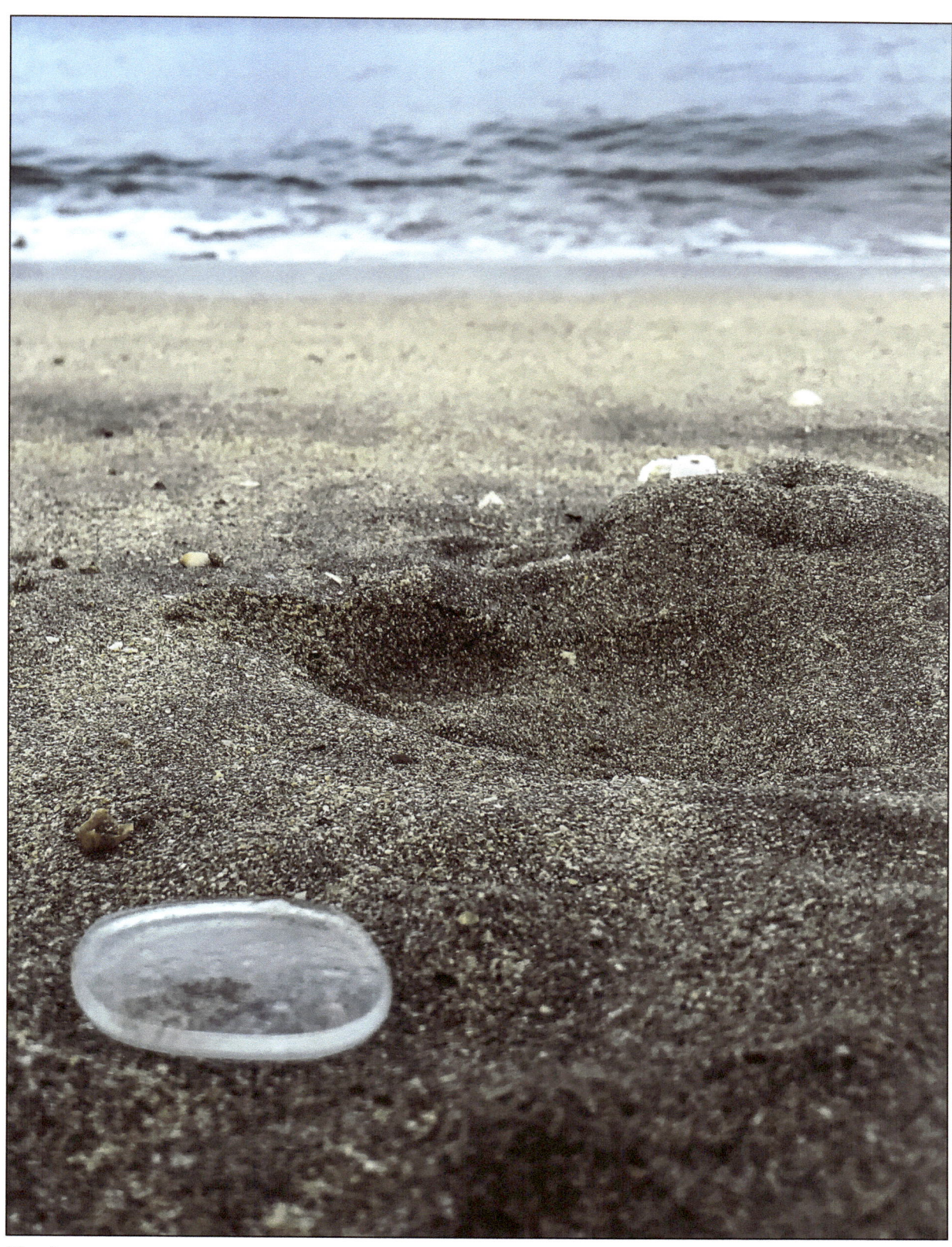

*Myopia*
근시

# Echo Beach

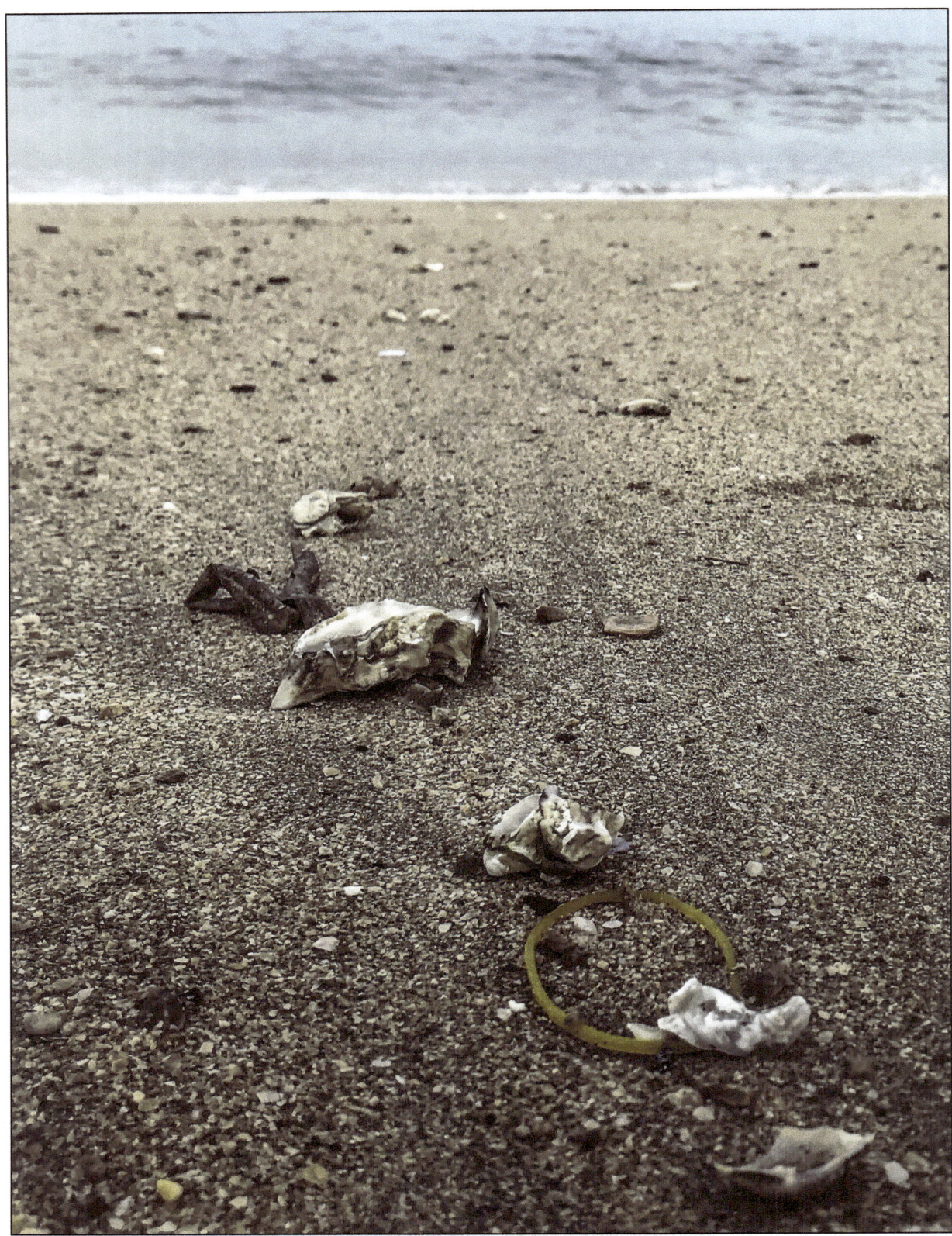

*Band of brothers*
형제 집단

*Seohae Mon Amour*

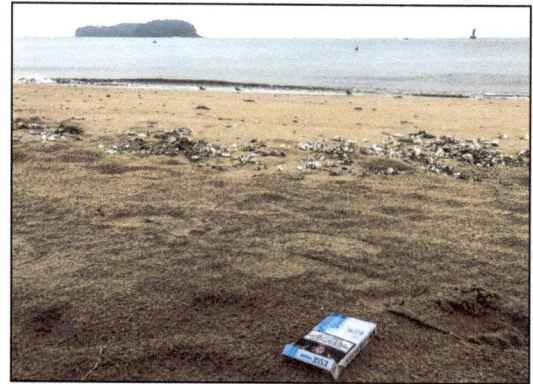

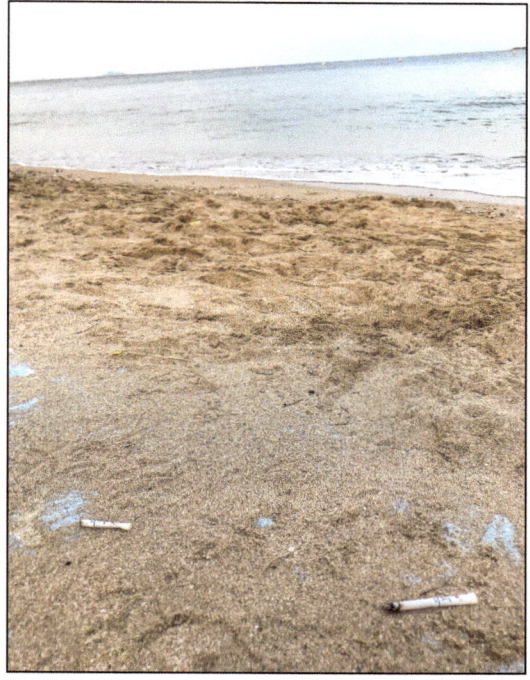

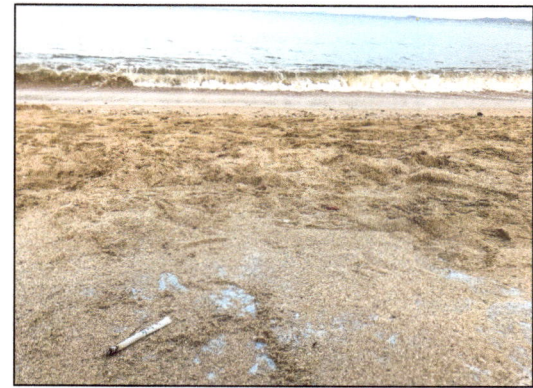

*Smoko*
짧은 휴식

# Echo Beach

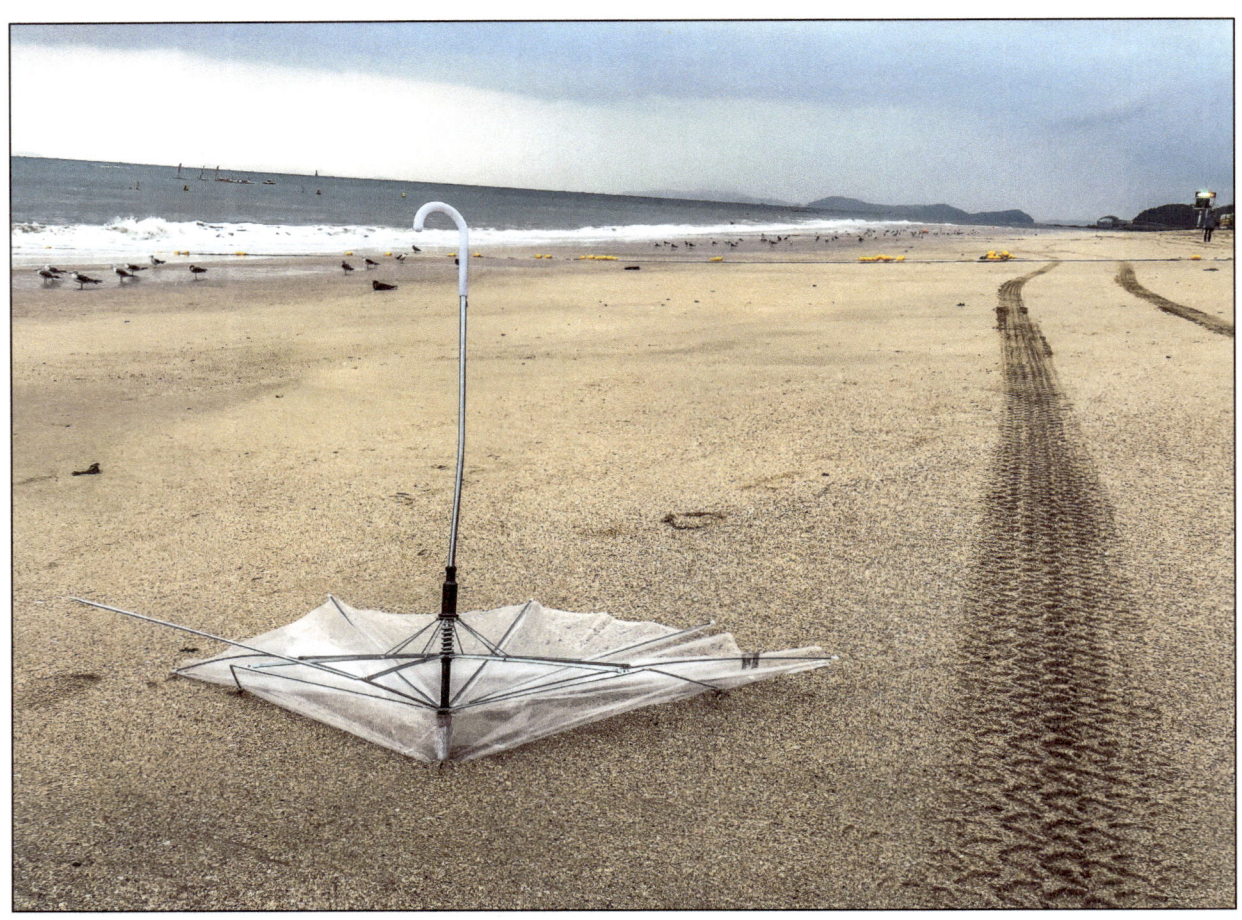

*Supercalifragilisticexpialidocious*
슈퍼칼리프래질리스틱익스피알리도셔스

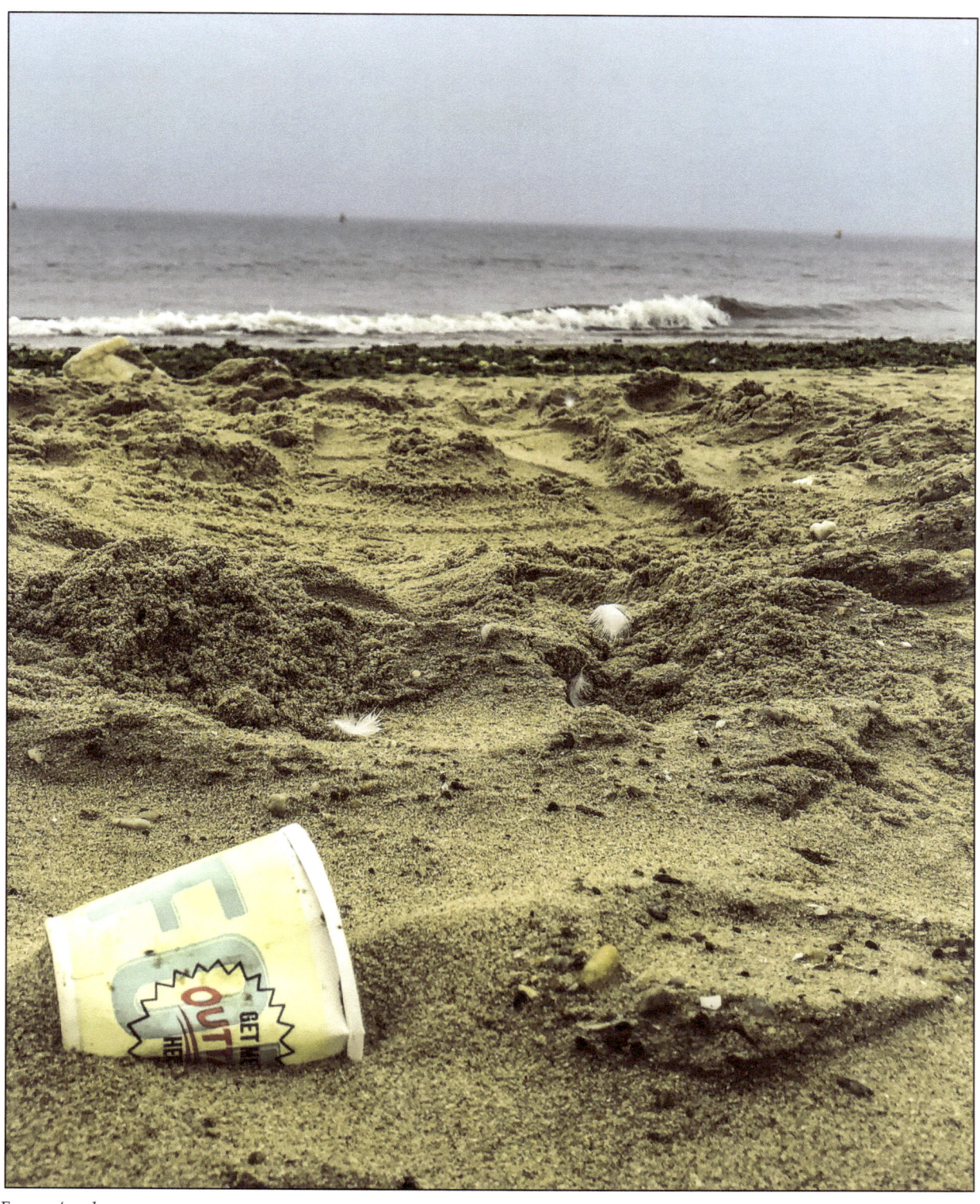

*For cup's sake*
컵을 위해서

# Echo Beach

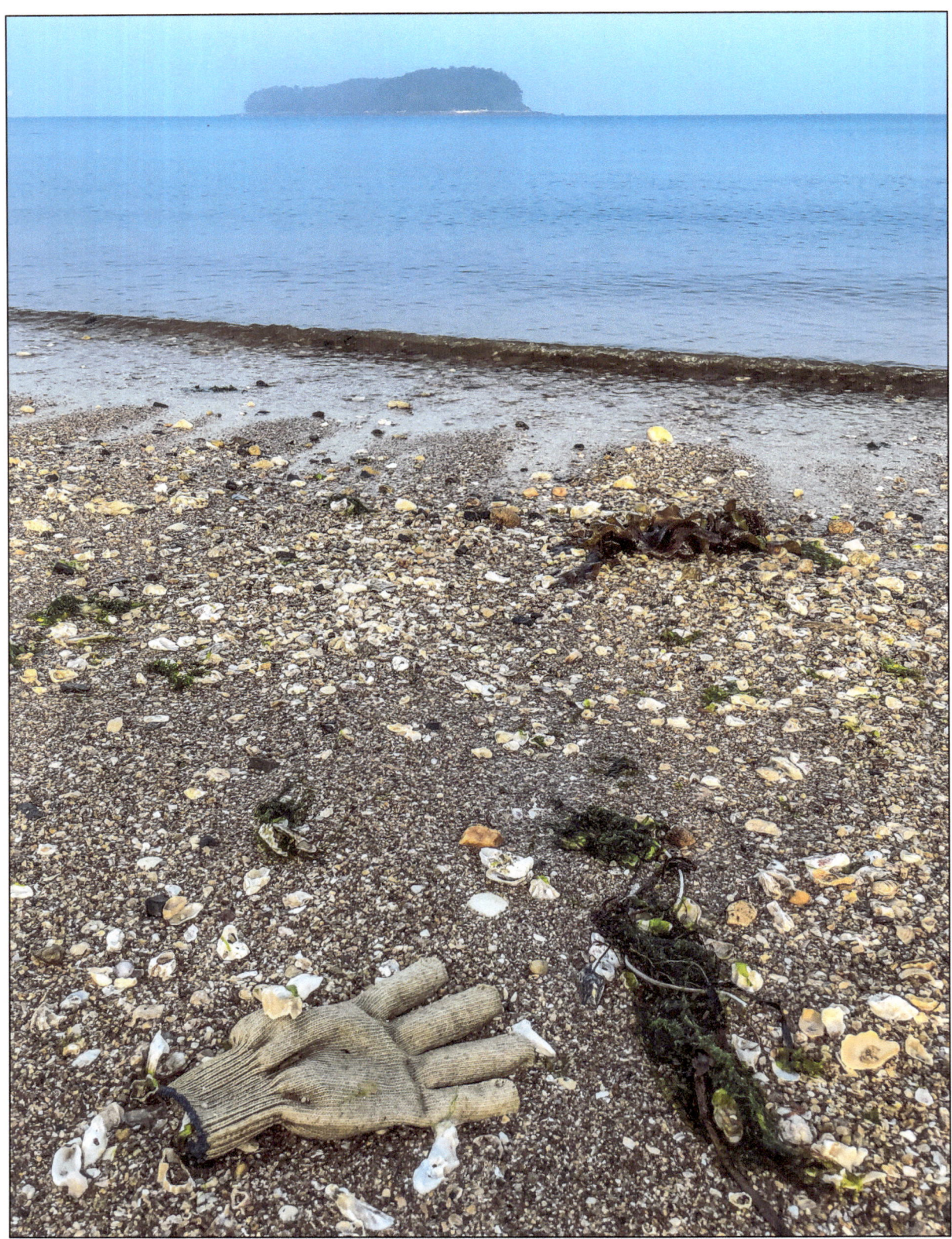

*Daddy's hand*
대디손

*Seohae Mon Amour*

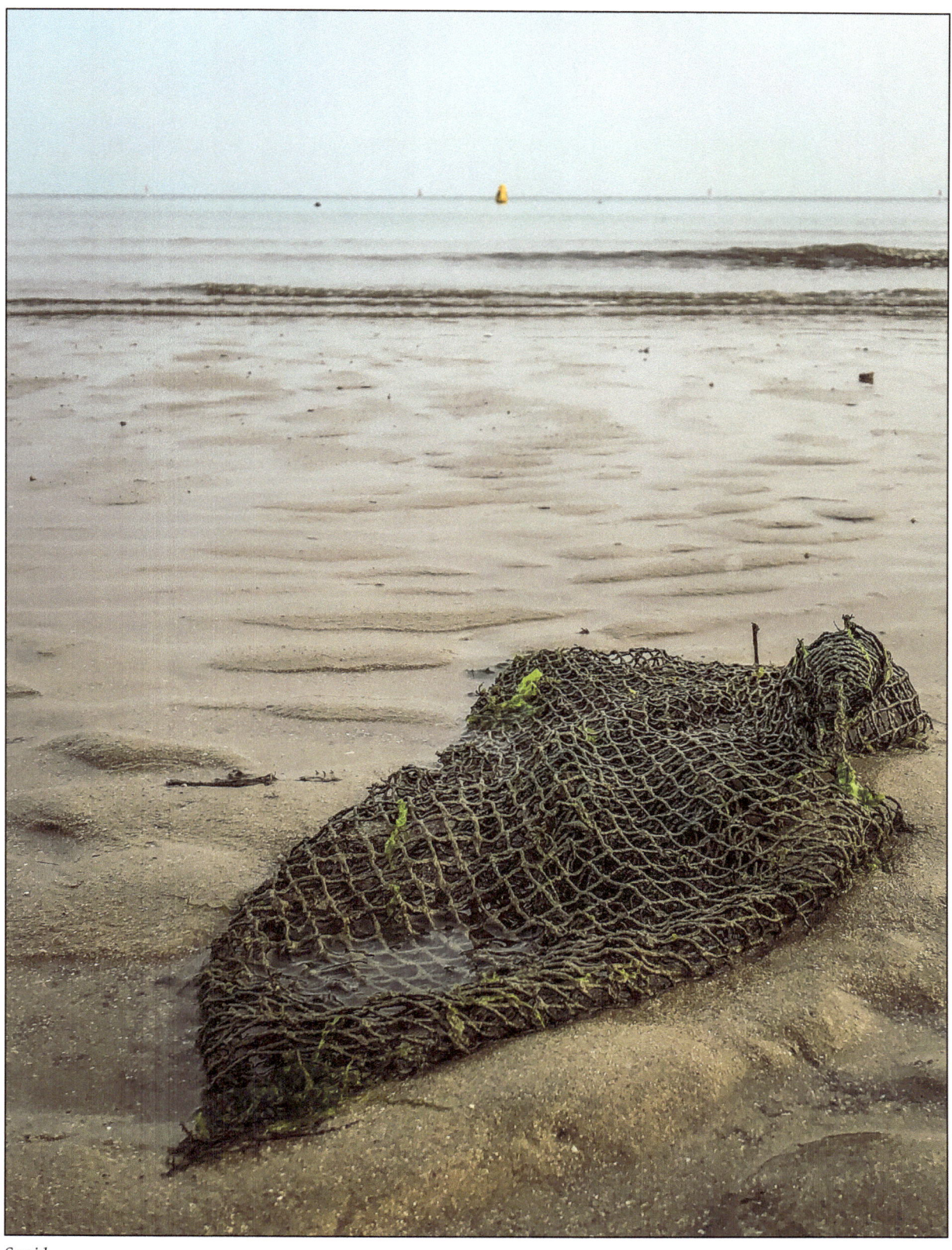

*Squid*
오징어

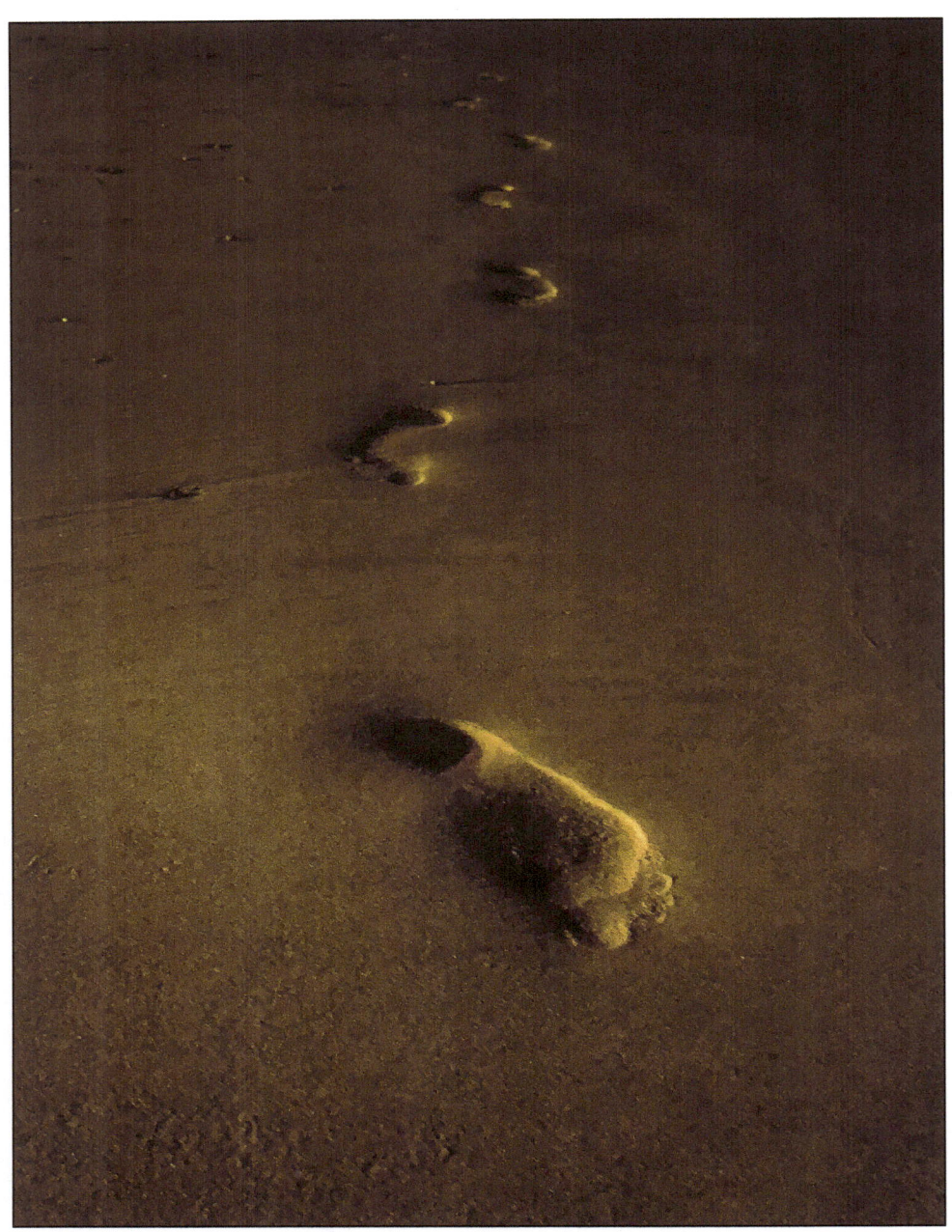

*One small step*
작은 한 걸음

# ABOUT THE PHOTOGRAPHER

David Kent (1973–) is an Associate Professor at Woosong University where he is also Head of Department and provides teacher education through the TESOL-MALL graduate program. Born in Australia and having grown up in Sydney, a harbor city, David now lives in Daejeon in the Republic of Korea with his family. He is a member of the Daejeon arts collective (DJAC).

## 사진사 소개

데이비드 켄트 (1973 년생)는 우송 대학교 부교수로 재직 중입니다. 또한 직위는 테솔몰 대학원 과정의 'Head of Department'이고, TESOL-MALL 대학원 석사 프로그램을 통해 사범교육을 하고 있습니다. 호주에서 태어나 항구 도시 시드니에서 자란 데이비드는 현재 대한민국 대전에서 가족과 함께 살고 있습니다. 그는 대전국제예술가모임(DJAC)의 회원입니다.

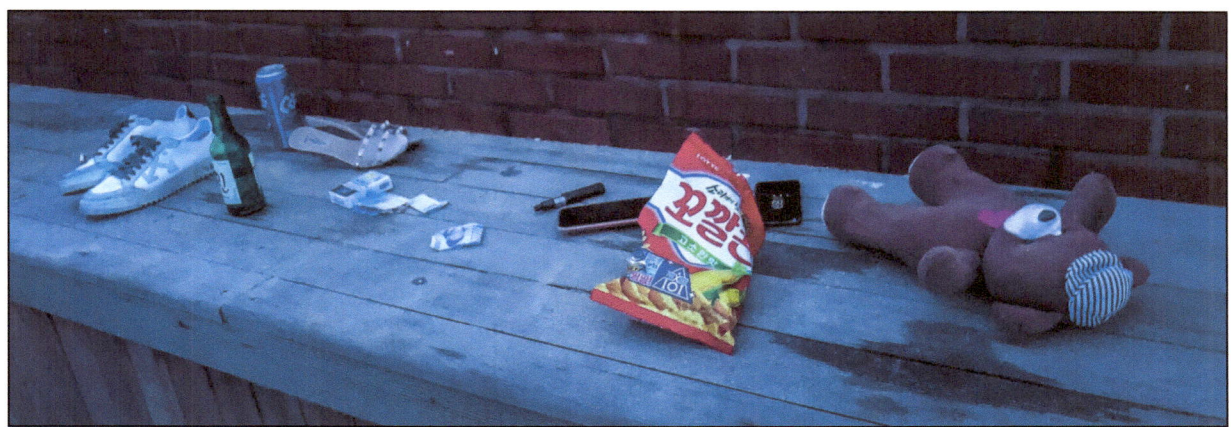

*Brown bear, brown bear, what do you see?*
갈색 곰, 갈색 곰, 너 뭐가 보이니?

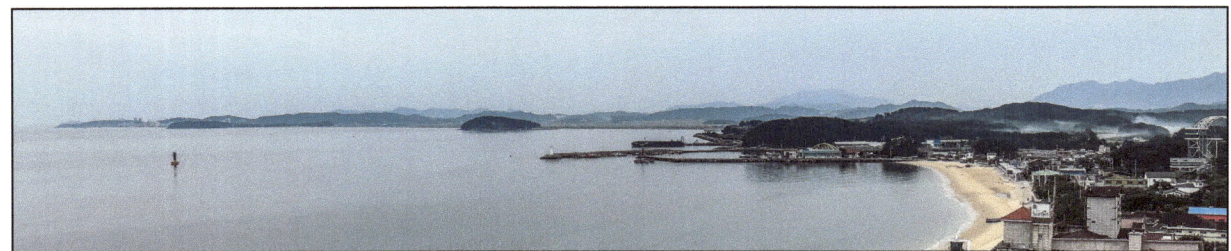

*Muchangpo*
무창포

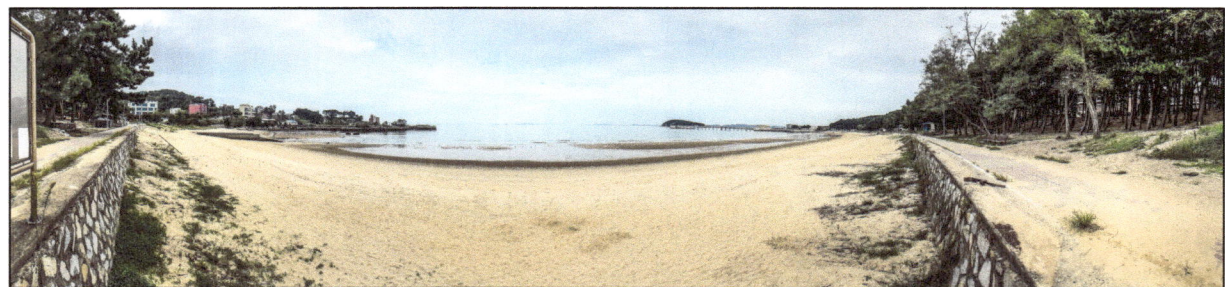

*Yongdupo*
용두포

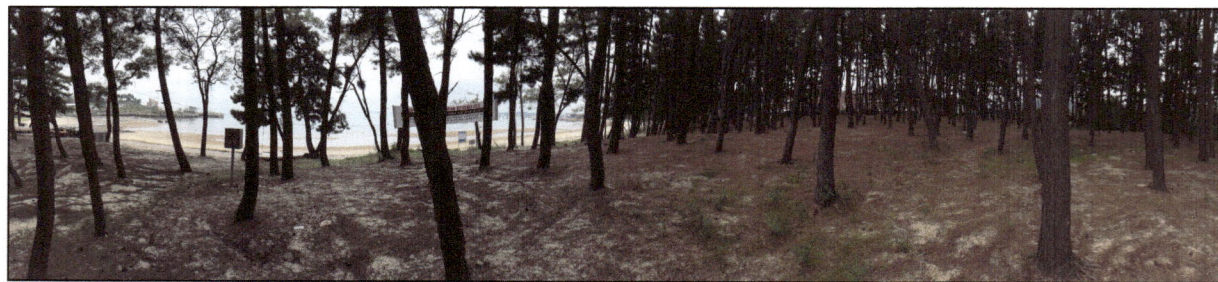

*Yongdupo grove*
용두포 작은 숲